COLLINS

COCKER SPANIEL

AN OWNER'S GUIDE

The authors

Lesley Scott-Ordish is the founder of PRO Dogs and the editor and main contributor to *Argos* magazine, which she started in 1976. She is the author of *Heroic Dogs*, and has contributed many articles to a variety of major publications and magazines. She is also a regular newspaper contributor to the canine specialist press.

Lesley makes many television and radio broadcasts and writes news releases about aspects of the work of the charities in which she has an interest.

John Bower BVSc, MRCVS is a senior partner in a small animal Veterinary Hospital in Plymouth, England. He has served as President of both the British Veterinary Association and the British Small Animal Veterinary Association. He writes regularly for the veterinary press and also for dog and cat publications. He is co-author of two dog healthcare books and a member of the Kennel Club.

Caroline Bower BVMS, MRCVS runs a veterinary health centre in the same practice as John. Her special interests include prevention and treatment of behavioural problems, and she lectures to dog breeding and training groups.

COLLINS

COCKER SPANIEL

AN OWNER'S GUIDE

Lesley Scott-Ordish

HarperCollins*Publishers*

DEDICATION

Dedicated to my sister Jane, who loves animals as much as I do,
and to my beloved Cockers, Ella and Tally.

First published in 1996 by
HarperCollins*Publishers*
London

A catalogue record of this book is available
from the British Library

ISBN 0 00 412799 4

This book was created by SP Creative Design for HarperCollins*Publishers* Ltd
Editor: Heather Thomas
Designers: Al Rockall and Rolando Ugolini
Production: Rolando Ugolini

Photography:
François Nicaise: front cover and pages 1, 5, 6-7, 9, 10, 11, 16, 17, 18, 20, 21, 26-27, 29, 30, 32, 47, 48, 50, 51, 55, 59, 69, 78, 79, 81, 83, 84, 85, 87, 90, 91, 93, 94-95
David Dalton: back cover and pages 3, 14-15, 24, 25, 31, 33, 34, 35, 38, 39, 40, 41, 42, 46, 49, 52, 53, 54, 57, 58, 61, 63, 64, 65, 66, 67, 68, 70, 71, 72, 73, 74, 75, 76, 77
Sally Anne Thompson Animal Photography: page 44
Lesley Scott-Ordish: pages 2, 19, 31, 37
Rolando Ugolini: pages 22, 64, 80

Acknowledgements
The publishers would like to thank the following for their kind assistance in producing this book:
Scampers School for Dogs for their help with photography, and special thanks to Charlie Clarricoates for all his hard work
Sally Cackett and her Cockers: Andy (Pinecourt Black Feather of Marldona) and Jaz (Bidston Mystery Jangles)
Carol Abbot and her Cocker, Amber (Windrush Lady)
Rolando Ugolini and his Cockers: Leo and Sam (Marldona Early Edition)

Colour reproduction by Colourscan, Singapore
Printed and bound by New Interlitho SpA, Italy

Contents

PART ONE – YOU AND YOUR DOG

PART TWO – CARING FOR YOUR DOG

PART THREE – HEALTHCARE

PART ONE

YOU AND YOUR DOG

The man and dog partnership has truly survived the test of time. No other animal has shared life so intimately with people throughout the world for so long, or has proved itself so useful as a worker and companion animal.

The dog has developed such a close affinity with man that he is readily trained to provide an impressive list of services for the benefit of people. No other animal has inspired the creative talents of so many writers and artists, and literature is full of generous tributes to much loved dogs.

The earliest existence of dogs is evident from prehistoric cave paintings, and the fossil remains of domestic dogs that lived over 12,000 years ago have been found in Iraq and Israel. Other fossils of almost equal antiquity have been found in many countries throughout the United States and Europe.

CHAPTER ONE

HISTORY OF THE COCKER SPANIEL

ORIGIN, DEVELOPMENT AND RECOGNITION

Looking today at the appealing Cocker Spaniel with his long ears sweeping the ground, silky coat and feathering, kept largely as a favourite companion pet, it may be difficult to see him as a willing working dog. However, the Cocker still has this ability and enjoys nothing more than the satisfaction of a day out flushing the birds, or at least a day in the country showing you where the last rabbit passed or where there is a nest in the hedge. Without the keen scenting ability of the dog, we pass by without noticing and miss so much on the daily walk.

Evolution of the spaniel

Spaniels originated in Spain and can be traced back to the fourteenth century. The name 'spaniel' may have been derived from the old French for 'Spanish' which is 'Espaignol'. Although this explanation seems to satisfy most breed historians, an alternative suggestion is that the name is derived from the old French term 's'espanier' meaning to flatten oneself or lie down. Certainly setters and pointers have the instinct to freeze when pointing game birds, but this explanation seems less satisfactory to describe how the name for spaniel came about.

As early as the fourteenth century a reference to 'spanyells' is also be to found in English literature and, at the risk of adding further confusion to this early research, it seems that the Irish may be able to lay claim to first using spaniels for hunting. This is because as early as 17 A.D. there is a printed reference in Irish laws to water spaniels as a gift to the king. However, Irish Water Spaniels are different in type and coat from other hunting spaniels.

By the seventeenth century a variety of different types of spaniel were gaining popularity as gun dogs in western Europe. Although the work of the dogs in flushing and retrieving game birds was basically the same, the variety of terrain and ground on which they worked and the different types of birds which occupied the habitat led to the need for several types of working dog. As a result

spaniels of varying size and type developed from one district to another.

Early in the nineteenth century, the prefix 'Cocker' was given to denote the popularity of this game little dog for flushing out and retrieving woodcock. The 'Cocking Spaniel' became popular in Wales and south-west England at that time due to his compact size which made it easier to work in low, dense covert.

The Cocker Spaniel of today is still a willing working dog and should not be deprived of exciting country smells.

EARLY POPULARITY

It was not until 1892 that the Kennel Club of Great Britain recognised the breed.This was really the debut of the Cocker Spaniel – the start of his rise in fame and popularity.

The Cocker has many attributes that contributed to his early popularity: firstly, his game and happy personality leading to his well earned description as a merry working dog. His compact size and pleasing appearance, coupled with his anxiety to please and trainability, made him a good working and domestic companion.

His enthusiastic and busy wagging tail as he hunts has the happy effect of lifting the spirits of those who walk or work with him, and his gentle, biddable disposition makes him an affectionate companion.

His flat and silky coat is a pleasure to stroke and caress, and many dog owners actually select a dog or breed of their choice based partly on the coat type, without always recognising the importance of this factor for them. Coat type should always be taken into consideration in choosing a dog, and this includes the amount of grooming and trimming required as well as the importance of tactile sense.

Stroking the lovely silky Cocker's coat is pleasurable for the dog, and a health benefit for the owner.

RECOGNITION OF THE COCKER

Summary of history of the Spaniel

- 14th century: spaniels originated in Spain
- 17th century: variety of spaniels emerge in Western Europe
- 19th century: prefix 'Cocker' given to smaller spaniels in the UK.
- 1892: Cocker Spaniels recognised by the Kennel Club of Great Britain

Dog owners can become compulsive strokers, to the mutual benefit of man and dog. In recent years, scientific research has shown that this instinctive stroking actually has positive health benefits. It causes lowering of the human heart rate, relaxation and reduction in stress: a tonic without the risk of unpleasant side-effects associated with some drugs! Now that heart disease is the main cause of death in many countries, including the United States and the UK, this is a significant power for good. Dogs enjoy it, too!

REACHING THE LIMELIGHT

Quite soon after World War I the Cocker Spaniel started to reach the limelight by a series of spectacular wins of best in show at Cruft's dog show.

Cruft's dog show is staged annually by the Kennel Club of Great Britain, although the two world wars and other factors left some gaps in the schedule. No show was held between 1918 and 1920 or 1940 and 1947, and it was not until 1928 that the much coveted award of best in show was staged. This is judged today from the dogs already selected over the period of the show as firstly best in their breed. The dogs assessed as best of their breed go forward to compete as best of their group. A representative of each

Tracey Witch of Ware, owned by Mr H. S. Lloyd, won the double crown by winning best in show at Cruft's in 1948 and 1950. (Cruft's was not held in 1949.)

group goes forward and the show is then brought to an exciting climax by judging the best dog in the final group to give an outright winner overall.

In 1930, and again in 1931, H.S. Lloyd's Cocker Spaniel Luckystar of Ware achieved the Cruft's best in show crown. Exquisite Model of Ware, also owned by H.S. Lloyd, managed the double Cruft's crown again in 1938 and 1939. After a break in the show between 1940 and 1947, the unbeatable Lloyd's Cockers returned again, and Tracey Witch of Ware won in 1948 and again in 1950. No other breed has ever matched this outstanding achievement.

Luckystar of Ware, owned and handled by Mr H. S. Lloyd, was best in show at Cruft's dog show in 1930 and 1931.

BREED GROUPS

Breeds are divided into groups by the Kennel Club of Great Britain, which is the governing body for registration of pedigree dogs, as follows:

■ Hounds	■ Utility	■ Gun dogs
■ Terriers	■ Working	■ Toy dogs

Cocker Spaniels are classified in the gun dog group. Kennel Clubs exist also in other countries to keep breed records and registrations.

BREED STANDARDS

Breed standards are devised by, and available from, Kennel Clubs of various countries. For any one breed they will vary only slightly from country to country. For example, the ideal height for a male Cocker in the United States (where it is called an English Cocker Spaniel) is 40-42.5cm (16-17in), whereas in Great Britain the height to aim for is 39-40cm ($15\frac{1}{2}$-16in). The standards are a description of what are considered by the experts to be the most desirable points, based on the working ability of the breed.

Tail
Still customarily docked (see page 24). The tail should be carried level and set on a little lower than the back. It should always be happy, merry and wagging in action.

Body
Compact with a deep chest and well-sprung rib cage. Wide but short loins and the top line of the dog sloping downwards slightly from loin to tail.

Legs
With good bone, strong and muscular. Short below the hocks on the hind legs to allow good, tireless movement.

Coat
A silky coat which lies flat. Good feathering on the chest, legs and belly.

Head
The skull and the muzzle are of equal length with a clearly defined stop mid way.

Eyes
Gentle and intelligent in expression. Dark in colour.

Mouth
Strong jaw and teeth with a scissor bite, i.e. with the teeth in the upper jaw closely overlapping the teeth in the lower jaw.

Ears
Set on low at same level as the eyes. Ear flaps long enough to reach to the tip of the nose, and well covered with silky hair.

Feet
Neat, compact and cat-like.

MALE DOG

A male dog should have two testicles fully descended into the scrotum. The testicles do not always both come down together, and they appear over a variable time scale of weeks/months so it is not always possible to be sure of this important point when buying a young puppy. Be very gentle when checking this point and, if in doubt, get your vet to check it out when you first visit. A monorchid (only one testicle) or dog with testicle retained inside the body can cause problems in the future and no attempt should be made to breed using a monorchid dog.

COLOUR – THE MAGIC OF THE EYE SPOTS

Cockers come in a wonderful and wide variety of colours. In fact, no other breed offers quite such a large choice. Solid or self colours include black, red, golden and liver. The red is often incorrectly described as golden, but the true gold is much paler than the typical red, and much rarer. Liver is also a comparatively rare colour, described by some people as chocolate.

In the solid colours, it is regarded as a fault if there are white hairs anywhere on the dog other than on the chest. **Particolour and tricolours** include any one, or variety of, the solid colours mixed with white to produce a flecked combination colour coat, and/or one with larger patches of colour.

Black and tan is yet another colour combination and these dogs result from mating dogs of solid colour which carry the tan gene. These dogs, as well as some of the tricolours, show the orange spot over the eye which ancient folklore in Tibet suggests gives these dogs magical powers of perception. They are supposed

Cocker Spaniels come in a wide range of colours, both solid and mixed, as illustrated below by these three dogs.

to be able to warn their owners of impending doom or disaster.

It is easy to dismiss such ideas as being nonsense, but having a remarkably sensitive and cute dog of this colour myself, I am almost persuaded. I have also carefully noted the many dogs with this feature that I have met over the years. Several dogs awarded medals for life saving or pet of the year in my book *Heroic Dogs* have these rather endearing orange spots above the eyes.

Black and tan and tricolour Cockers sometimes have distinctive orange spots over their eyes.

2

What price popularity?

Guardians of the breed

You may think that the increasing popularity of the Cocker and the growing demand by the public for puppies of this appealing breed would be joyous news to the breeders. Not so! Breeders tend to set themselves up as guardians of the breed in which they have a strong interest. Cocker Spaniel clubs exist in many countries, and in 1995 there were twenty four registered breed clubs for Cockers in the UK, from the Black Cocker Spaniel Society to the Yorkshire Cocker Spaniel Club. These clubs have a considerable influence on their members and the

Many puppies born now will not live to see their first birthday in their original home, often due to problems with house-training and behaviour.

PAT DOGS

A comparatively new service provided by dogs with their owners is the PAT Dog hospital visiting scheme. Over 8000 dogs in Great Britain are used regularly to visit lonely people. They provide a welcome contact with the outside world and bring friendship – at a stroke! Here PAT Dog Ella, with the author, visits an elderly patient in hospital.

breed and are involved in promoting names of breeders they consider suitable for judging lists.

Show dogs

In the world of show dogs, the most influential members are exhibitors one week and judges the next. Judging of any dog is always against the breed standard, but interpretation is a matter of personal opinion and it is not always easy for the exhibitor or bystander to understand how or why the winner of any class has been chosen. It is not like watching a race where a clear winner can be declared.

However, at some shows, there is a star quality in a winning dog which cannot be denied. The dog is such a typical example of the breed and so proud of himself that he obviously enjoys the crowd and the fun of the performance. It is a joy to watch him cover the ground. The audience is clearly behind the personality of such a show dog and usually in these circumstances there is a clear winner and a satisfied audience.

The demand for puppies

But what about these guardians of the breed? Why should they be so concerned about a growing demand for puppies? The answer is that the breed becomes so important to these enthusiasts that they are reluctant to see the wholesale spread of dogs and puppies into the hands of the non-expert, or pet owner. They want to retain enough control, even after the puppy has ben sold and gone to its new home in some cases, to ensure the future welfare of the dog. Maintaining a good relationship with the breeder after sale can be beneficial provided that the initiative to get in touch is left with the puppy owner, in case of need.

Follow-up advice can be helpful in getting a puppy clean in the house, and maybe at the destructive puppy teething stage. These are two phases that can be difficult for a first-time owner, and large numbers of puppies fail to remain in their new homes by the age of twelve months. When the man and dog relationship has failed once, a young dog is likely to have picked up habits which will make it more difficult to retrain. Once the decision to own a dog has been made, wherever possible it is better to overcome any difficulties that may arise with expert help to avoid the unhappy steps leading to a dog that nobody wants.

In the UK, the PRO Dogs National Charity has a 'Better British Breeder' scheme whereby after-sales service is promised and all necessary certificates are provided at the time of sale, including a certificate of worming showing that a puppy has been treated and is fit for family life. While every care is taken to advise new owners before the puppy goes to its new home, in case of failure the breeder will have the dog back (see the

GENETIC FAULTS

It has to be said that sometimes even the most experienced breeders of Cocker Spaniels have unwittingly been party to the introduction of some genetic faults. It is not possible to breed without this risk. The good stock breeder takes the finest examples of his breed and line breeds them to stamp the good points on the offspring. Unfortunately in so doing he also multiplies the risk of bringing out any faults from this limited gene pool which would have been less likely to show up in unrelated parents.

All breeds are at risk from inherited faults and, contrary to popular belief, mongrels and cross-breeds can suffer from such conditions too. As breeding records and pedigrees are not normally kept for non-pedigree dogs, such conditions are not recorded and no plans are made with the aim of eradication in future breeding programmes.

Cocker Spaniels look immensely appealing and are a joy to own. They make rewarding companions, and any puppy behaviour problems can usually be overcome.

Useful Addresses at the end of this book).

Some Cocker breeders may also be concerned at what they see as the risk of the superb qualities of a popular breed being reduced in the hands of non-expert breeders who may be willing to breed without due care and knowledge of faults which inevitably creep into some breeding lines. This can happen when there is a sudden big demand for puppies.

Behaviour

The most typical and most widely appreciated characteristic of the Cocker Spaniel is the happy friendly nature of the dog and his willingness to please, making him an ideal companion dog. I have personally always found that my Cockers are a joy to look at and a pleasure to be with.

However, back in the 1930s the occasional Cocker began to appear with a far from typical temperament. The problem seemed to be confined to dogs of solid colour. Yes! Those hot headed red-heads were to blame again, but also some solid black Cockers.

Rage syndrome

My very first Cocker Spaniel, waited for longingly for many years until I could have her, was actually one of those dogs inflicted with a degree of this so-called 'rage syndrome' although I did not recognise it or know about it at the time, back in 1953, when she was purchased.

The way in which the problem showed itself was in her hiding away in the kitchen behind the boiler and by barking in an angry and untypical manner. This behaviour was usually provoked by a visitor, but sometimes occurred spontaneously. Although she was not happy at these times, we had a great relationship and when I insisted on pulling her out from her safe place and picking her up, to stop the noise, she would never have dreamed of turning on me or biting.

Nevertheless, I would not recommend this method of handling an unhappy dog

The typical red Cocker Spaniel is still a reliable and delightful companion, but there is a temperament problem in a small number of dogs of solid colour.

to others. The way you hold, comfort and support is everything. My dogs always seem to be mesmerized by, or 'addicted' to the way I cuddle and stroke them. This means that if they are injured or in pain they still allow me to handle them in any way necessary.

The small percentage of Cockers suffering from this rage problem are basically unreliable and they can easily misinterpret moves and gestures made by their owners, particularly if the relationship between the family and the dog has been confused. An arm suddenly raised to read a newspaper may seem to an unbalanced dog to be a threat from which he needs to defend himself. Dogs always give prior warning of attack, but you always need to be tuned in to the body language of your dog to be one step ahead of him, or even to notice the warning at all. Watch the facial expression and be warned by a very slight curling of the lip.

I do not believe that dogs affected by this have any control over these episodes. Afterwards they may seem bewildered, disoriented or apologetic.

DOGS IN SOCIETY

The outlook for unreliable dogs in society today is not favourable and dogs with behaviour problems must always be kept under control in public.

BE PRUDENT

There are still plenty of reliable, sound and delightful Cockers around but it is prudent to be aware of the rage problem before buying a dog, so that questions can be asked about any known manifestation in the dog's line.

Such dogs should never be left with children and for safety's sake should learn to wear a correctly fitting muzzle in public. The plastic open-mesh cage type is kinder than the snug-fitting type and the dog will have to be very slowly acclimatized to wearing it.

Researching a cure

The guardians of the breed are understandably distressed that such behaviour should have crept in to this breed, noted for its gentleness and tolerance, and the London Cocker Spaniel Club has spent considerable time and effort in raising funds needed to support research by Cambridge University. Work will be done to see if any genetic factors can be found and identified. This will be a valuable follow-up to work already done to isolate the possibility of medical causes. None have yet been found, but the effects of epilepsy and degeneration of the central nervous system, at one time considered a possible cause, have been studied.

DOCKING

Docking is still a controversial issue as far as the custodians of the breed are concerned and likely to remain so for some time, so the debate may be of interest to owners as well as a point to consider before obtaining a puppy.

Although the standard for the breed still states that tails are customarily docked, in 1973 the Royal College of Veterinary Surgeons in Great Britain decided that dogs do not benefit by having their tails cut off and that it was unethical for vets to dock litters of puppies for cosmetic reasons.

Furthermore, in 1991 an amendment to the Veterinary Surgeon's Act brought in a clause making it an offence for breeders or any lay persons to continue to dock tails. However, in Europe and the United States, the tails of Cockers are still docked.

The new UK laws have not had the immediate effect of preventing tail docking that was intended. The subject continues to be controversial amongst the traditional dog breeders who do not want to see the fashion changed. A great deal of energy has gone into preserving

The author's dog, 'Tally', kept her natural tail, even before laws aimed at preventing docking were introduced in the UK in 1993. In celebration, her name is 'Trendsett Happy Ending'.

WORKING DOGS

It is argued that working dogs can suffer tail damage if left undocked, but I never had this problem. Although dogs will certainly adapt themselves to the loss of their tail, as they will also to loss of a limb if it has to be amputated, the best interests of the dog are served by allowing it to keep its natural tail which it was provided with and born with for good reason.

If you have seen a dog swimming, you will be aware of how important the tail is as the rudder for balance. On land, moving at speed, the natural tail is used to help swift changes of direction. The docked dog takes much longer to turn and is therefore at a disadvantage here. As one Cocker I bought some years ago was docked when I had her, I have been able to observe and compare dogs with and without tails.

Just as dogs used to be hobbled to impede movement, it was suggested in 1920 by a Captain Jocelyn Lucas that spaniels, intended for hunting game but not for catching it, originally had their tails cut to disadvantage them and hold them back. The tail is also needed for signalling messages either to other dogs or to observant owners. Wagging the tip end of the tail, the part removed by docking, is a warning of nervousness and anxiety.

A main concern of the pro-docking lobby seems to be that a good show dog will now have to be judged on tail carriage in addition to other points, and tails have not had to be considered or bred for in the past.

the status quo and lobbying to find vets who can still be persuaded to dock.

Since personally coming back to owning Cockers again after so many years with beloved English Setters, I have never permitted Cockers I have bred to be docked. Setters have such beautiful natural flags and I could see no reason why the Cockers should not also enjoy natural tails. Despite warnings that Cockers with tails would never sell, the general public were keen to have them.

However, perhaps Cocker owners will take heart from the action of the breeders of Cavalier King Charles Spaniels. This breed had docked tails until some breeders themselves decided to stop docking in the mid-1940s. Now Cavaliers have beautiful natural tails as part of the picture.

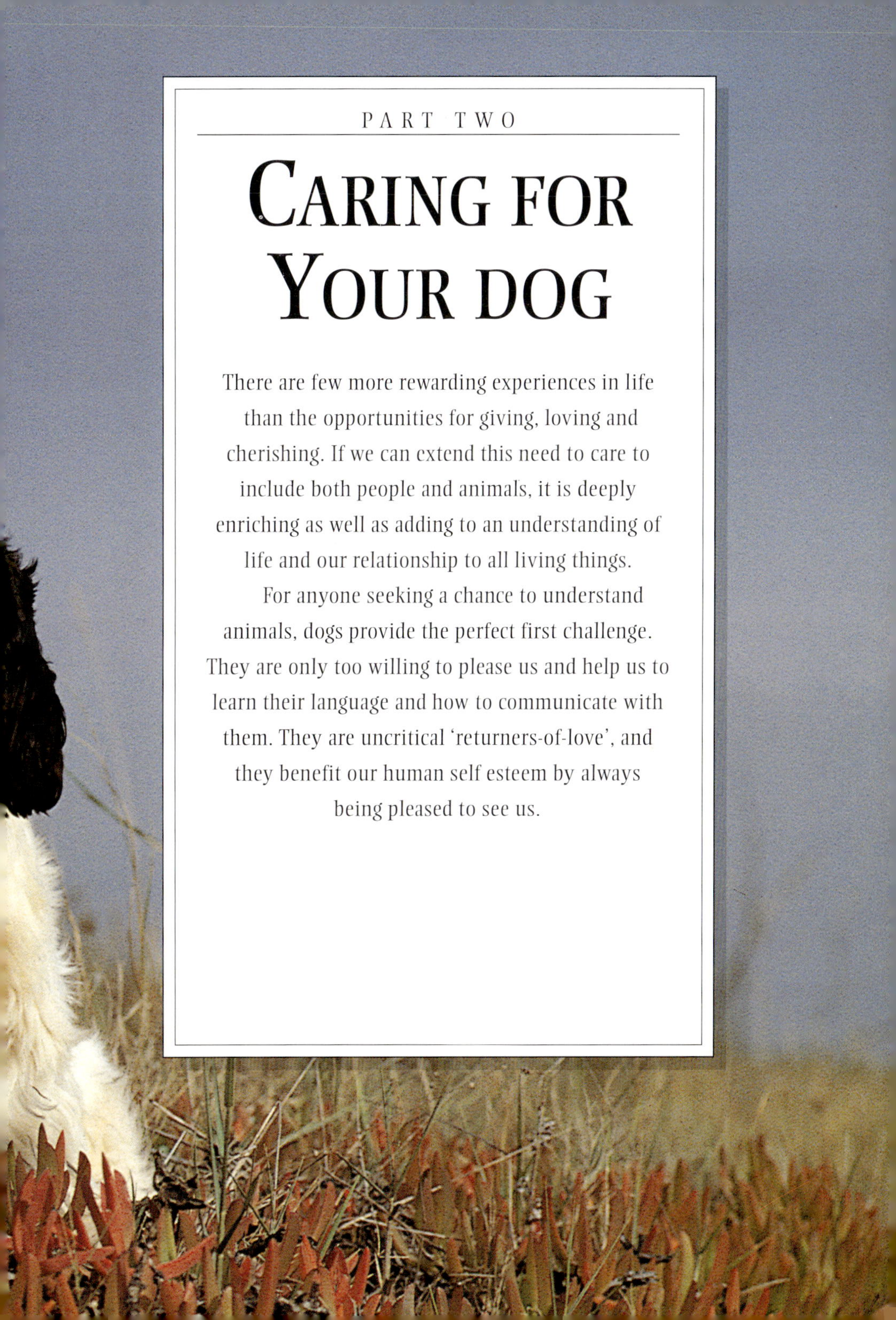

PART TWO

CARING FOR YOUR DOG

There are few more rewarding experiences in life than the opportunities for giving, loving and cherishing. If we can extend this need to care to include both people and animals, it is deeply enriching as well as adding to an understanding of life and our relationship to all living things.

For anyone seeking a chance to understand animals, dogs provide the perfect first challenge. They are only too willing to please us and help us to learn their language and how to communicate with them. They are uncritical 'returners-of-love', and they benefit our human self esteem by always being pleased to see us.

CHAPTER THREE

YOUR PUPPY

WHERE TO BUY

A beautiful and friendly dog is always a pleasure to own. In choosing a new puppy you will be looking for a close companion to share your life for the next twelve years or so. It is therefore important to take all the time and trouble necessary to select from the most promising and reliable sources.

Finding your ideal source

■ Dog shows

It is well worth a visit to a local dog show or two where you will have the chance to see a number of Cockers and meet some exhibitors and breeders. If you watch the judging for a while you will be able to select the dogs that appeal to you. If you buy a catalogue of the show, this will give you the names and addresses of all the exhibitors, and a walk round the benching area where dogs are waiting to be shown in their class will provide further information. Occasionally you may even see a sign that puppies are expected shortly from various kennels.

■ Magazines and canine papers

You can find out when shows are being held in your area by obtaining copies of the weekly canine papers. The useful address section at the end of this book (see page 144) will give you contacts.

PUPPY SOURCE	
Hobby dog breeder, breeding the occasional litter with the aim of producing a good show/working dog for his own hobby interest	**Good/ideal.** Probably house reared. You will see pups with mother
Larger scale breeder specializing in one breed only	**Good.** Probably see both parents but dogs may be reared in outside kennels Less human handling
Breed rescue centre	Usually older dogs only
Pet shop	**Not recommended**
Local vet or own personal research	**Can be satisfactory**

■ Vets and friends

Your vet may also be able to recommend to you a local breeder. Alternatively, from personal contacts and research with your friends you may also find a good source by tracking back to find the breeder of dogs that you know and admire.

■ Breed rescue centres

The breed rescue societies provide another source, but usually for older dogs. Dogs can be in rescue for a number of reasons: maybe the owner has died without leaving other provision for the dog, or the domestic circumstances of a family have changed so that there is no longer anyone at home to look after the dog. The most likely reason is that the previous owner was unable to cope with the dog who may now have developed some difficult habits.

Good rescue centres and societies will be able to give you an assessment of a dog and will ask a lot of questions before letting you have one. In any circumstances, a disturbed dog is going to need lots of patience and animal understanding to overcome the past sorrows and difficulties he may have faced. Although meeting and overcoming the challenge can be reward in itself, the first-time dog owner would probably be better advised to start with a puppy. Yes! Even though it means coping with getting the puppy clean in the house! This is usually quite quickly achieved.

WHAT TO LOOK FOR IN CHOOSING A PUPPY

Having patiently identified a suitable likely source for your puppy, what points do you need to consider in order to negotiate a promising purchase?

Before you make an appointment to visit the litter, it may be helpful to list some of the points you need to clear and questions you want to ask. Almost certainly the breeder will have an equal number of questions for you, before agreement can be reached on both sides.

Questions you may be asked

Caring breeders will assure themselves either that there is someone at home to be with the dog in the daytime, or that work facilities are relaxed enough for the dog to go to work too – more offices are making dogs welcome these days. Breeders may also want to remind you of the benefit of having a safe garden, or at

Puppies are blind at birth but by two weeks of age they are starting to open their eyes. It is not a good idea to visit pups as young as this. There is always a slight risk of taking infection in to the litter and some bitches are very protective towards the puppies. It is unfair to put them under stress.

Four-week-old puppies, sitting up and taking notice. At this age, they should be handled daily by the breeder.

least an area of garden which is fenced off, from which a puppy cannot escape.

Questions to ask

- You will want to get a firm agreement on the price being asked for the puppy and whether a deposit is required before you collect the pup, which is usual. If you pay cash, make sure that you receive a receipt.
- The puppies will be weaned gradually from their mother's milk by the age of five to six weeks of age, and it is advisable to ask for a puppy diet sheet so that you can obtain similar food to avoid a sudden change. Four meals a day are usual at about eight weeks of age.
- You will want details of pedigree and to be sure that the litter has been recorded by the breeder with the Kennel Club. Without this facility you will be

unable to transfer the ownership of your dog officially to your name. You will be unable to show the dog in your own name, should you wish to do so, and you will be unable to register any progeny if you ever decide to breed from your dog.

■ It is important to enquire tactfully about any known inherited diseases or problems and whether the sire and dam of the litter have been examined or tested to reduce such possibilities. Most caring breeders are good about providing all this information, perhaps before you've even got round to asking.

Observing the puppies

There is a great deal to be learned by just watching the puppies. They should be warm and contented. This may sound obvious, but don't buy from a litter if the pups are thin and unhappy and perhaps showing evidence of discharge from the eyes or ears.The mother will also tell you a great deal. Her teats may still be a little

In the next three-week period, the puppies develop very quickly. They enjoy playing with their litter brothers and sisters and start to learn how to interact with them. This is a good age at which to visit with the aim of selecting a puppy.

WHAT TO LOOK FOR IN A PUPPY

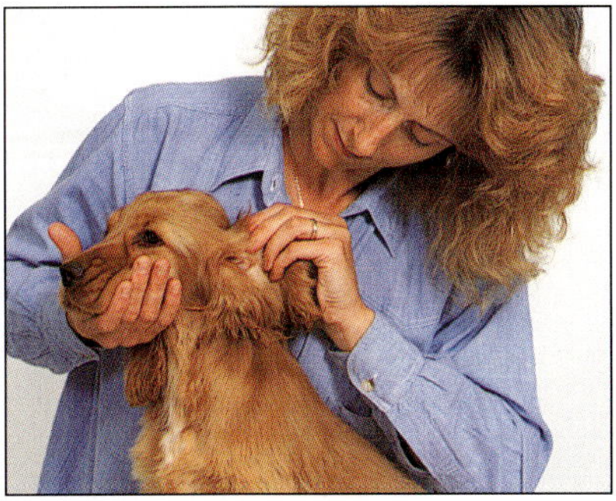

1 Gently fold back the ear flap to note any ear wax.

2 Note the darkness of the eye and general expression.

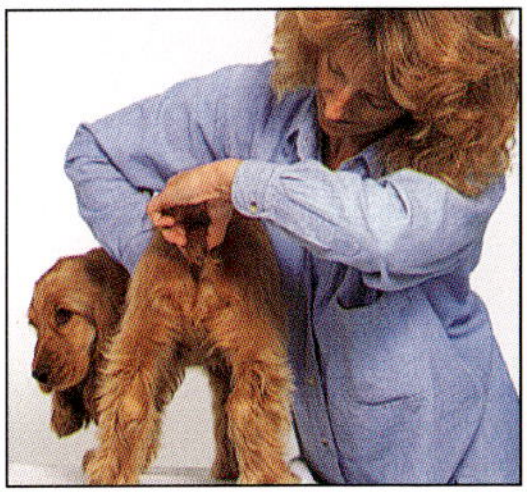

3 If buying a male puppy, gently feel for two descended testicles and, for both sexes, check for bulge indicating umbilical hernia.

4 Check for correct bite (see page 15), although adult teeth and jaw growth may change the bite with maturity.

heavy and uneven, if her milk has not yet quite dried up, but apart from that she should look well fed and cared for. If, when you talk to her gently, she greets you by lying submissively on her back and urinating just a trickle you should be wary of this sign of nervousness. This is not typical behaviour of the bright and merry little Cocker – even if she is feeling protective of her babies.

The breeder may feel five weeks is too young an age to sort out the likely show prospects if the litter has been bred with the aim of showing. If you have an interest in showing, you may wish to ask the breeder for a likely show puppy, but expect to pay more for it. However, there is never any guarantee that the dog will achieve what looks like early promise. Breeders have been known to let a pup go to a pet-only home, to discover later that this was the most promising in the litter after all! So you can take your chance and choose entirely by your own instincts and observation. You may find that you have an eye for a show puppy to vie with the experts.

DON'T FORGET

- Ask for a diet sheet
- Get a receipt
- Ask for details of pedigree
- Inquire about any known inherited diseases
- Study the pups carefully
- Look at the mother too
- Stroke the puppy and play with him
- Let the puppy get used to your scent

Smell is very important to dogs, and your human smell will be quite different from the family he is used to so let him have a chance to get the scent from your hand before you pick him up. Take your time and play with him and stroke him while he is still on his familiar territory.

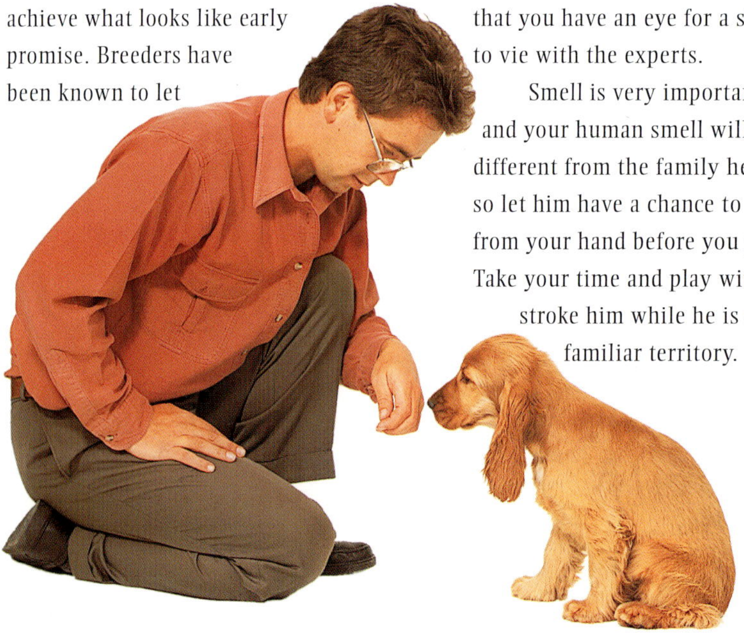

PICKING UP A PUPPY

The way in which you hold your puppy will have an important influence on how quickly he feels confident and safe with you. Support him as shown.

1 Place your hand underneath the puppy to take the weight.

2 Hold the puppy firmly and confidently, and talk to reassure him if he is unused to being lifted.

3 Another way to hold a puppy, is with the paws falling in between your fingers.

CHAPTER FOUR

PREPARING TO BRING YOUR PUPPY HOME

EQUIPMENT AND TOYS

Although it is unnecessary to buy all the equipment you may need before you bring the puppy home, there are some essentials you must have.

The first decision to take is where the puppy is going to sleep. It is very important to provide a safe den where the pup can see what is going on, learn the everyday sounds of life but be protected. A puppy play pen with mesh panels, open at the top, is ideal for this and can be bought at larger pet stores.

The floor should be covered in newspapers, which can be burned easily and then replaced. It's as well to start collecting these in advance. You may find that the pup is already toilet-trained to using newspapers when you get him.

ESSENTIAL EQUIPMENT

- Puppy play pen
- Bed with washable pad
- Toys, e.g. tug toys
- Nylon chew bones
- Collar and lead
- Feeding bowls
- Grooming equipment
- Identity disc
- Puppy food

Puppy den

Inside the puppy's den will be his bed with a comfortable washable pad on which he can sleep. Puppies are so destructive in the first few months while they are teething that it may be wise to delay purchasing a proper dog bed. Even the strong nylon and plastic types soon become ragged with sharp edges after the determined efforts of some young dogs! Cardboard boxes from the supermarket can provide temporary accommodation, covered by a pillow case, with a sleeping pad inside. Firm boxes also are fun objects to climb on and, with an opening cut in one or two sides, they make tunnels to

Ella loves her comfortable bed, which is all washable. However, she had to wait until she was past the puppy chewing stage before she got it!

This is an ideal safe place for a puppy. He will learn to feel secure quite quickly in his restricted pen, where he can watch everything going on around him.

rush through, or hidey holes. Put them down for play periods only, while you are around, to avoid cardboard being chewed. Puppies eat anything and everything, as you will discover.

Toys

Puppies are great fun to play with and they will quickly be stimulated by toys.

- An excellent variety of safe toys is available now. Chewable toys, such as the 'kong', made from tough rubber-type material, are the best toys for the puppy play pen. Dogs will chew contentedly on these for hours.
- Nylon chew bones and toys are also popular and are useful in helping to keep teeth clean and healthy. They are a particular comfort to teething puppies.
- Other toys are fun to play with outside in the garden. Dogs always love to chase a ball, but make sure the ball you choose is well made, solid and too large to swallow.

■ Frisbees provide an alternative for the older dog who can become adept at judging direction and catching.

■ Cockers particularly like to have a favourite toy to carry around in their mouths and love to 'offer' these to you in pleasure in welcoming your return. If you don't provide proper toys, they will find their own offerings to bring, such as tea-towels, shoes or anything within reach! It is important to allow them to exercise their natural carrying instinct.

■ Tug toys made of knotted rope or plastic-type pull toys are fun for two dogs playing together, and toys with a squeak in the middle encourage dogs to pounce and attack them. But the most favoured toys for Cockers are the ones to retrieve and carry around. For example, my dogs like old socks which have been washed and stuffed tightly full of other socks and knotted or sewn up at the top. These make ideal soft dummies to find and retrieve – and they cost nothing.

The range of toys for dogs has never been more extensive. Be selective in your choice and get toys out for a special playtime treat for the dog to enjoy. They should not be left around, but put away after playtime so that the dog really looks forward to this special time and does not get bored playing with the same toys.

A selection of toys and retrievable objects providing hours of pleasure and stimulating play for your dog. They include a 'kong', playbell, solid ball and tug all made from hard rubber, firm and soft dummies for retrieval training and a frisbee.

EQUIPMENT TIP

Buy a soft leather puppy collar and a strong lead. You could invest in an extending lead for easier training.

Collars and leads

- A soft leather collar is a good choice for a first puppy collar. However, the pup will grow out of the first size relatively quickly so it is not worth buying a very expensive one. A nylon ribbon-type collar is a good alternative. You will not need a check chain collar to train a Cocker and they are much too severe to ever use on a puppy.
- A leather lead is a good investment. It will not get outgrown and with use will become supple and pleasant for the handler to use. The clip on the lead is important and should be checked and examined before purchase to make sure it is robust and cannot release itself. Rope leads are also available but you may find that they slip and are far less comfortable on the hand.
- An extending lead is a most valuable aid in training. It gives the dog additional space in which to run while you still have control of the lead.

Feeding bowls

There are some feeding bowls available which are well suited to coping with the problem of avoiding getting food all over your Cocker's ears at meal times. Small-sized bowls with sloping sides are good for ensuring that ears stay dry. However, you may find that ceramic oval pie dishes are helpful for small pups.

You will need to have clean drinking water available all the time, and the best drinking bowl for Cockers is the plastic type with a fitted lid, leaving only a small drinking space in the middle with room for the face, but not for the ears.

Choose a feeding bowl that will enable your Cocker's ears to stay dry.

COLLARS AND LEADS

1

2

3

1 A heavy chain lead. This may not be suitable for your Cocker spaniel.

2 This fabric lead is preferable, although a leather one is better still.

3 A heavy rope lead. Again, this is probably not suitable for your dog.

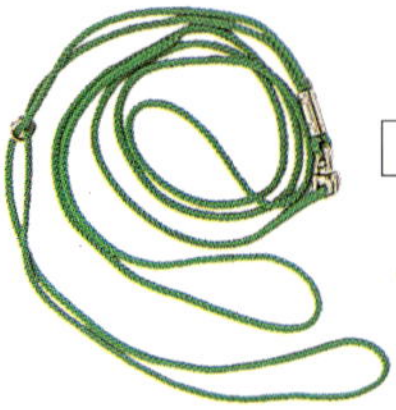
4

5

6

7

8

9
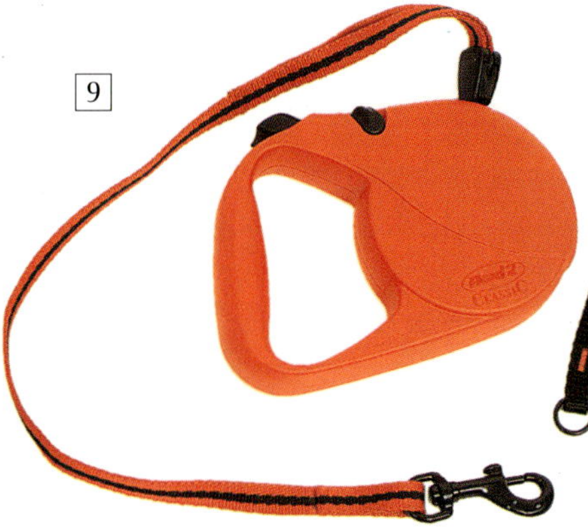

4 A lightweight puppy lead.
5 A narrow nylon collar.
6 A suitable leather collar.
7 & 8 Fabric collars.
9 An extending lead.
10 Fabric slip choke collar.

GROOMING EQUIPMENT FOR PUPPIES

You will need a brush, comb and scissors which are suitable for the Cocker coat. A small bristle brush is best for the soft coat of a puppy, and a comb with metal teeth will be needed to deal with any tangles on the ears or feathering, as he grows.

In addition to these, you will need some thinning scissors and another pair of scissors to trim round the feet.

Your puppy will quickly grow to enjoy grooming time, which should be made as pleasant as possible. Try to combine plenty of stroking and touching your dog with brushing and very gentle combing.

METHODS OF IDENTIFICATION

In some countries, including Great Britain, there is a legal requirement for dogs to be identified when outside their own territory by a disc on their collar, which is engraved with the owner's name and address. Other less common methods of identification are listed below.

Microchips

Some organizations advocate inserting a microchip into the neck of the dog with an identification device in it which can usually be read by a monitor. However, there is understandable resistance to putting a foreign body into a companion animal and at the time of writing the availability of 'readers' is restricted and the chip itself has not been standardized to a single type. The main problem is not knowing, without a 'reader', whether or not a dog is carrying this internal identification or not. Some devices have failed and some dogs have been implanted with more than one chip when the first one failed to show up on the scanner.

The device has to be inserted into the scruff of the neck of the dog by a vet using a needle of substantial size, although the microchip itself is about the size of a (large) grain of rice.

The idea of a means of identification that cannot be removed is attractive in some respects, particularly to those dealing with stray, lost and unwanted dogs. It may also be welcome as a useful source of income by vets. However, it would have to overcome a deal of legitimate resistance and the concern of dog owners if it was ever to be made compulsory. Although there are several types of chip, there is no European standard at present.

Tattoos

An alternative means of more or less permanent identification is by tattoo: a system that has been used for many years for racing greyhounds. This is done either in the hairless inside flap of the ear or inside a back leg. It is carried out by tattooists who do not need veterinary qualifications which makes the cost less than for the implant of a microchip.

IDENTITY DISCS

It is a fact that collar discs can be lost, stolen or not provided but it seems a more appropriate general means of identification for our companion animals. Which method of identification would your dog choose? Get a disc engraved now and then attach it to your dog's collar as soon as possible.

Safety factors

For peace of mind, there is probably nothing more important to the dog owner than a secure garden, or an area of garden from which even a small puppy cannot escape. Strong wire mesh fencing or wooden fences are important, and careful attention must be paid to secure locks and gates. Puppies can slip under some gates with ease, so, if necessary, add mesh to the bottom to prevent this.

The cost of fencing is considerable and if you have a large garden you could consider making just a small area dog-proof and allow the dog into the rest of the garden only when you are present. In this case, make the secure area adjacent to the house/back door.

This puppy, with his expressive undocked tail, is going to have to learn that good dogs must not 'stalk' the flowers!

There will be many occasions when the dog needs to go out and it may not be convenient to have to lead him to the far end of the garden!

If there is a pond in the garden, this should be covered to avoid accidents. Other garden hazards include chemicals and insecticides, e.g. slug pellets have caused many serious accidents to dogs. If you use these, keep them under lock and key in a garden shed.

Grasses and herbs

- Where dogs usually have a great deal of sense and natural instinct is in the selection of natural grasses and herbs that they need. Provided you know the source to be clean, either from your own garden or fields that you are quite sure have not been chemically sprayed, you should permit your dog to eat these finds which you may have noted have taken some time to seek out.
- So many owners reprimand their dogs and snatch the grasses off them because they do not want the dog to be sick. However, the dog probably needs to be sick and carefully chooses the grasses that will make him vomit because there may be unhealthy irritants in the stomach which will be brought up at the same time as the grass.
- I always leave a little couch grass in the garden because sometimes if the dogs are out of sorts they will seek out this little patch to make themselves feel better. We have lost so many of our own natural sensitivities and instincts, but we can re-learn much by respecting the instincts of animals. It is easy to lose a sense of perspective and discount the value of the relationship between animals and man. Dogs keep us in touch with our roots and place in nature which our over-populated, grasping society sometimes makes us forget.

POISONOUS PLANTS

Unfortunately many garden bulbs, shrubs and plants are poisonous to dogs, and puppies in particular seldom have the sense to leave them alone. Beware of: azalea, arrow grove, bayonet root, burning bush leaves, cyclamen, caster beans, dumb cane weed, hemlock, elephant bar, foxglove, jimson weed, laburnum (seeds and pods), lily of the valley, locoweed, mistletoe, monkshead roots, mock orange blossom, narcissus bulbs, peach, elderberry, cherry trees (bark), pimpernel, poinsettia, rhododendron and rhubarb leaves, a plant known as four o'clock (root or seed), sweet pea (stem), scotch broom seeds, tulip bulbs and wisteria.

It is as well to be aware of which plants can be unsafe, but I have to say that many of the above list are included in our garden which has been a safe home to many dogs over the past almost thirty years. Our dogs have instinctively left them alone.

THE NEW ARRIVAL

All preparations are in hand and at last the day has come to collect the puppy. If it is to be a long journey by car it is worth considering buying a dog carrying box which will also be useful on future journeys. Choose the size for an adult Cocker spaniel. Line the floor of the box with newspaper and put a soft towel on the top with more spare towels and paper in the car as well as some drinking water and a bowl. If this is the first time the pup has been in a car he may not be very happy about it and will probably be sick.

- Take the travel box in with you when you collect the puppy and leave it for a short time in his familiar play area, allowing his mother and any other puppies to sniff in and around it. The box will then have the friendly smell he is used to when you wedge the box back firmly inside the car, pup inside, making sure it will not move about on the journey.

Reasssuring the puppy

This will be a frightening experience for your puppy, away from his mother he

Cockers, 'Tally' and 'Ella', are safe in this suitably-sized travelling cage.

has known since birth and his fellow pups and familiar surroundings. He will need a lot of comfort from you to help him settle in and he should not be left on his own to cry.

■ Talk to the puppy reassuringly and introduce him to his safe den area. Try to encourage him to be interested in a toy and play with him. If there are other animals in the household for him to meet, let them wait until he is asleep in his den and then they can come in and sniff around. Established pets may be jealous of the new puppy, so let them get to know each other slowly and do not leave the animals alone together until you are certain that they are safe.

HOUSE-TRAINING

The best method of quick house-training is to let the puppy use newspapers in the house to start with. You have already put papers down in his puppy pen and it is likely that he also used newspapers at the kennels.

After meals

■ Every time a puppy wakes up and after every meal he will need to urinate, so these are the ideal opportunities to establish good habits by placing the pup on some paper or taking him to a chosen spot in the garden if it is not too cold or wet. The secret of success is always to wait with the pup until he has obliged and then praise him. He will learn quickly if you are patient with him.

Picking up the signals

■ A young pup of eight weeks has a small bladder and has to empty himself every few hours so there are bound to be some unplanned puddles and messes in the early days. Never scold a dog for mess after it has happened as he will not associate the mess with your obvious displeasure, even if you point it out. You will simply confuse him and this makes training more difficult. If you catch the puppy in the act, then you can say 'no' and immediately carry him to the approved spot.

■ If you watch your puppy, you will soon pick up the signals that he is about to empty himself. He will sniff around on the ground and may rush about. If you see these signs, then act at once, or you will be too late!

■ Use a neutralizing disinfectant in the house to clean up accidents and to prevent the area used from becoming a favourite spot for your puppy to return to again and again!

TOUCH AND USING HANDS IN TRAINING

Your hands are going to be able to teach your dog a great deal about you and what he needs to know in order to be a good companion to you.

It is vital that your puppy learns to love your hands and therefore you should never use them to punish him. Your hands are to stroke and reward and to provide two-way pleasure for both you and your dog.

If you have a touch-sensitive dog, and, in my experience, most of them are, you are a good way towards getting your dog mesmerized by the pleasure of being stroked! He will enjoy it so much that he will do anything you wish provided he understands your simple and consistent demands. Titbits may be useful training aids but touch is better.

It is possible, though difficult, to make a dog behave the way you want him to but this is likely to involve harsh methods and even bullying. The sensitive dog will shrink in fear of the trainer who has ways of making the dog behave. The object of successful training is to make the dog want to behave as you wish. The secret of success here is kindness and reward.

Reward your puppy in training with touch and gentle praise. Only give titbits occasionally.

WHAT'S IN A NAME?

One of the first things your puppy needs to learn is his name, and some people devote much study to thinking up a good name for their dogs.

The registered Kennel Club name of the dog may, or may not, be a good starting point if you wish to choose a similar-sounding name. For example, a dog I registered as Trendsett May Queen was known throughout her life as Queenie, while Trendsett Solo Dancer was always known as Solo.

You can learn quite a lot of the ambitions and views of breeders by going through a breed year book. Masterpiece may indicate pride in a dog regarded as a man-made creation, whereas Nature Boy might suggest a thought for going at least one step back to nature, and perhaps breeding a Cocker with slightly shorter ears, which do not get so tangled and interfere with his work. 'Ard to Match and Best of the Bunch are perhaps names hopefully given to try to impress the judge when writing up the critique! Then there are quaint names, sometimes including a courtesy title, and the challenge of trying to create a name that is going to be unforgettable.

However, the only thing that really matters is to choose a name, perhaps of two syllables, that trips easily off the tongue and makes for easy calling. The list is endless and you can even buy books on naming dogs if you need some other ideas to inspire you.

Once you have chosen the name, the puppy has to get used to the sound of it, and he has to associate the calling of his name with an immediate need to respond and come to your hand for reward. His name should be used or called in a pleasant and encouraging voice, always with a pleased response from you when he answers. Therefore, if you have to say 'no' to him to caution, warn or admonish him, do not say 'no, Freddie', because this gives him two opposite and confusing messages. 'No' means 'I mustn't do it' or 'I've done something wrong' and 'Freddie' means 'I'm a good boy and must go for my cuddle/reward'.

CHAPTER FIVE

FEEDING AND DIET

PET FOODS

Not so many years ago, keeping and feeding a number of large dogs usually meant finding an obliging slaughter house or knackers yard. It was necessary to maintain a good relationship with them in order to be kept informed about reliable sources of casualty meat and nutritious offals.

It also meant keeping a large chest freezer for dog meat supplies only and a wash boiler which could be plugged in, hopefully somewhere away from the house. This was to cook up the noxious raw green tripes and some of the other meat. Cooking smells were dreadful but the dogs thrived on it, especially with the addition of wholemeal bread or boiled rice and an occasional food supplement, plus lots of raw vegetables.

A well-balanced diet will keep your dog fit, energetic and healthy.

New laws and hygiene regulations have closed this source of supply, which was no doubt welcome news for the pet food manufacturers.

Manufactured pet foods

Good balanced diets have been studied by the pet food industry over the years and brought to a fine art, having been tried and tested on generations of animals. Now the dog owner does not even need a can opener to prepare the dog's dinner. Cans have ring-pull tops, and an increasing number of dogs are fed dry, or semi-moist complete dog foods.

- The high-protein canned foods are generally mixed with dog meal to provide the correct balance, and the manufacturer's guidelines should be read and followed.
- Some owners may find it hard to feed their dogs an unremitting repeat diet of a complete dog food. However, the manufacturers assure us that if the dog never has anything else he will thrive, and his owner will have a convenient and simplified feeding time.

VEGETARIAN DIETS

Dogs are not true carnivores and enjoy raw fruit and vegetables if they are offered from an early age. My dogs have always liked sliced apples, raw carrots, raw cauliflower (including small quantities of the green stalk), raw cabbage and runner beans. If the produce is not fresh from your chemical-free untreated garden, all vegetables need to be well washed first.

Some vegetables, such as peas and beans, and foods including soya products, are not able to be fully digested by enzymes in the digestive system of dogs, so they pass undigested into the large intestine where they may ferment and cause some flatulence.

A growing number of people are turning to vegetarian food and may wish to consider this diet for their dogs. Dogs can certainly survive on a vegetarian diet, but this is not a basically normal regime for them. Additives will be needed, and a correct balance of proteins, fats, carbohydrates, vitamins and minerals maintained. It may be helpful to consult a pet food manufacturer who produces vegetarian food for dogs. For more information, refer to the useful addresses at the end of this book (see page 144) or ask your vet for advice.

All dietary requirements are included in these foods, we are told.

Water

It is essential to remember that dogs need fresh water available all the time and this is particularly vital for dogs limited to a complete dry food diet. I have to say that I have some personal reservations about recommending this diet for Cockers as occasionally they suffer from kidney disease and a moister diet may be better. If you are attracted to the ease of these diets, write first to the manufacturers, as they usually have a specialist animal dietician and can be most helpful.

If you make a habit of refilling the drinking bowl at the same time each day, you will be able to note if and when there is an increased thirst and demand for extra water. This can be a warning sign of health problems and a matter that should be reported to your vet.

A selection of popular dog foods. Moist, prepared canned foods (top) and all-in-one pellets (below) are the 'convenience' dog foods of today.

YOUR DOG'S IDEAL WEIGHT

It is estimated that more than twenty five per cent of the dog population today is overweight, and an obese Cocker Spaniel is certainly not a pretty sight! In addition, carrying too much weight is a health risk to your dog, just as it is to people. Obese dogs are at increased risk from heart disease as well as certain types of cancers. Their life span is shorter, they are less mobile and more at risk of digestive problems.

Obesity can be caused as a result of neutering and/or hormonal imbalance and older dogs tend to put on too much weight because it becomes increasingly difficult for them to move about and get the exercise they need.

It is useful to have a monthly weigh-in for your dog because his weight can increase almost imperceptibly, and this will help you to catch the trend quickly while it is still easy to correct.

There is one sure, certain way to prevent any weight increase and that is by reducing the calorific intake of the dog.

Have a monthly weigh-in to check the weight of your adult dog, and a weekly one to ensure that a young growing dog is making good progress. Keep a weight card, or write down the dog's weight regularly in a diary.

WEIGHING YOUR DOG

A fully grown Cocker should weigh about 12 kg (approx. 26 lb) and the easiest way to weigh your dog is first to weigh yourself on the bathroom scales and then weigh yourself again, holding the dog. Deduct your own weight from the second total.

LEFTOVERS

Many families will have leftovers from their own meals and not wish to waste them. Any meat, carefully boned fish, poultry, vegetables, eggs, pasta or boiled rice can be put in the refrigerator and served with the next dog meal. Be careful not to include any bones from meat or poultry, but bone-free giblets and poultry or game skin can be included.

Such a hard thing to do, to ignore those adoring, appealing Cocker eyes, but it pays to be firm. In the first place, it is better never to start a habit of titbits offered after you have eaten your meal or between the meals of the dog.

Plenty of dogs manage quite well with a single meal each day, although my experience is that two meals are better. It is the quantity that counts! I feed a small breakfast of crunchy biscuits and an evening meal of meat, mixer and vegetables, including selected leftovers from the family dinner.

Allow the dog only a short time, say ten minutes, to clear his dinner bowl. If there is the competition of other dogs or pets fed at the same time, five minutes will be plenty of time! But a lone eater may become fussy, especially if he thinks he can return to eat later. A time limit may sharpen his appetite.

Working dogs have greater energy needs and will require extra calories dependent upon the nature of the work and how long they are working. Kennel dogs living in unheated surroundings will also need more than the basic outline above, as they burn up more energy to keep warm in colder weather.

YOUR DOG'S DAILY REQUIREMENT

To supply their daily energy needs, Cockers require about 900kcal each day if they are getting at least an hour of walking plus play/ exercise time, and if they are living in the house. However, dogs are individuals and only experience will show whether more or less than this is required to maintain the ideal weight.

An intake of 900kcal is achieved by feeding the following:

- 1 x 400 g (14 oz) can meat plus 145 g (5 oz) biscuit or biscuit meal, or
- 180 g (6 oz) semi-moist food, or
- 225 g (8 oz) complete dry food

Note:
These recommended quantities are intended only as an approximate guide to feeding your dog, and deductions will need to be made to compensate for any home cooked leftovers, if they are offered. Divide the quantity to provide the daily ration if two meals are given to your dog.

FEEDING GROWING DOGS

The calorific needs of a growing dog are much higher than those of an adult dog. No change should be made to his diet when he is first brought home, and the breeder's diet sheet should be followed. It is likely that the puppy will be fed four meals a day at this age, but by four months three meals will suffice. The stomach of a puppy is small and he cannot take in sufficient nutrients for his growing needs unless he is fed little and often.

■ Puppies need to grow rapidly from weaning to about six months of age. The growth rate then slows a little. See the feeding guide (below). Always read the manufacturer's information provided on the pack or can.

Milk

'So what about milk for puppies?' many people wonder. But the fact is that cow's milk is not a particularly valuable food for dogs and can give puppies diarrhoea. Goat's milk is nearer and a more suitable substitute for bitch's milk, although by six weeks of age the puppy should have taken what he needs of this most valuable start in life.

■ Warm milk, or milk and water, can be used to soften the puppy biscuit meal to make it easier for young puppies to take.

HOW MUCH TO FEED YOUR PUPPY

A guide to the quantity of canned meat and biscuit you should give to your puppy (based on 400 g (14oz) cans of meat prepared for puppies).

2-4 months	4 cans plus 110 g (4 oz) biscuit divided into 4 meals
4-6 months	1 can plus 150 g (5 oz) biscuit divided into 3 meals
6-9 months	$1^1/2$ cans plus 225 g (8 oz) biscuit divided into 2 meals
9-12 months	1 can plus 150 g (5 oz) biscuit divided into 2 meals

Note: Cooked rice, scrambled eggs and wholewheat cereal can make useful additions to the diet, especially in elderly Cockers.

FEEDING THE ELDERLY DOG

At the other end of the age scale from the puppy, special consideration also has to be given to caring for ageing and elderly dogs.

Old dogs that have given a lifetime of pleasure and service usually have a serene and endearing quality. They also have to endure increasing difficulty in moving about, and perhaps failing senses. They can be an expense if they require increased veterinary attention to make them comfortable, but they bring out the nurturing quality in people and the opportunity to provide the extra care and attention needed.

If you are fortunate enough to have your dog still after twelve years, he will need to be fed two or even three meals a day. The total quantity given is likely to

Scrambled egg is nourishing food for the elderly dog.

need to be reduced to compensate for the diminished exercise he probably takes. Little and often is once again the rule.

Care may also need to be taken to provide nutritious but easily digested foods, such as boiled rice with chicken or scrambled eggs. This diet is easy to eat but some hard biscuit or dog chews should still be offered to help keep the mouth clean. It is not possible to make any hard and fast rules about elderly dogs. As with people, some dogs age better or more slowly than others.

At this time in his life, the ageing dog needs extra care and attention including increasing his meal-times, but not the total overall quantity, to provide a 'little and often' diet.

Socializing and Training Your Dog

The importance of socialization

Puppies often miss out on a vital period in their lives when they ought to be learning about the big world and how to interact with people and other animals. This is because it coincides with the time at which young dogs need to be protected by vaccination against distemper, hepatitis, leptospirosis and parvovirus. Most vets advise that puppies should not be allowed to go out and mix until after completion of the course.

The age at which vets vaccinate dogs varies, but some courses are not complete until the dog is fourteen or sixteen weeks of age, and the all-important initial period for socialization has already been lost. The scientists Scott and Fuller, after extensive work on the development of dogs, pinpointed sixteen weeks as the age at which the socialization period ends. So what are you to do?

You are advised to follow the recommendation of your own vet in the matter although I have to say that I have allowed my puppies to mix with certain other selected dogs and people during this crucial period without any ill effect and with positive benefit.

THE 'SIT' AND 'COME' TRICK

The easiest way to teach basic commands is by a simple trick. You tell the puppy to sit just as he is about to do it anyway. Hold him gently and briefly in the sitting position while you repeat 'sit' and 'good boy' once more, so that he gradually learns to associate the sitting position with the command. Teaching a dog to do what he wants to do anyway is a certain recipe for success.

CAR TRAINING

It is to be hoped that if the pup's first car experience was on the journey home, this has not put him off car travel too much! It is important to put him back in the car the next day for a minute or two, without even moving the car if he is unhappy. Words of praise and comfort and the distraction of a toy may be helpful.

■ You should progress to short journeys as soon as the puppy is reasonably content, and, as you drive, reassure him. Dogs vary considerably as to the length of time they take to adapt to car travel without car sickness, but with the little and often treatment they do get used to it. Indeed they learn quite quickly that the car usually means something to look forward to with a walk at the end of the ride.

■ Always carry drinking water, a bowl and towels, tissues and clean-up bags in the car. Owners have a responsibility to clean up after their dogs in public places and there are many scoop-up products now on the market. However, small plastic bags saved from the shopping are equally suitable if you check that they have not got any punched safety holes in them first!

Hot weather

■ It is worth providing blinds in the car for summer weather to reduce sun glare for passengers and dogs alike during travel.

■ It is never safe to leave a dog in a stationary car in hot weather. Not even for ten minutes. The rate at which the temperature increases is alarming even if the car is in the shade when you leave it, and you accept the risk of theft by leaving all windows partially open.

The dog has no means of reducing his bodily temperature by sweating, as we do. His heat adjustment system was designed to cope with heat in open spaces where he can seek out shade and cover. In a baking hot car, as his temperature rises, he can rely only on this single inadequate system of panting, to help. He cannot take his thick coat off! Dogs have been known to cook to death in twenty minutes in a hot car. Don't ever risk it.

■ There is much you can teach the young dog at home from the age of eight weeks. The most important thing is to build his confidence by gentle kindness so as to establish a good relationship as early as possible. The puppy needs to feel safe with you.

You can teach 'come' in the same manner, as he approaches you. Use his name as well as the command and make it a fun game by taking a few steps backing away from him so that he wants to catch you for his reward. If you fall into the trap of chasing after your dog when you want him, you will be teaching him to run away from you. At meal times, let him see his feeding bowl and repeat the command 'come' so that he again associates his response to this command with something he likes. Again, you can take a few steps away from your puppy so that he learns to follow you.

Command your dog to 'sit', just as he is about to sit anyway. The hand signal indicates 'stay' in the sit position. Praise him by tone of voice and touch.

LEAD AND COLLAR TRAINING

Dogs do not enjoy being restrained by collars and leads. Why should they? But they have to learn this lesson to oblige us and make it safe to take them out of the garden. Again, patience is needed. Give them as long as it takes.

Your puppy needs to become familiar with his collar, which he may dislike to start with, and he must get used to what it feels like to have a lead attached. Make progress slowly and be patient. Training should be no more than a pleasant activity you enjoy together, and two minutes at a time, repeated later in the day, is plenty while he is young.

Walking on the lead

■ It goes without saying that a reluctant pup should never be forced to walk on the lead by dragging him along. For the first few days, put on his collar and attach a very light lead and let him get used to dragging it around for a minute or two. Then pick up the lead and encourage him to walk along happily by holding a toy in your hand. When he is fully accustomed to walking with you round the garden on the lead, you can progress to using an extending lead which will be useful in further early training.

■ In these early lessons, you will be giving the puppy basic training in walking to heel. He should walk on your left-hand side on a slack lead and you may need to start this lesson by keeping his interest with a toy or titbit in your hand, by your side. Never tug him back if he pulls forwards. He may tug all the harder. Instead, call his name and turn and walk in the opposite direction. Turn again, if necessary. Reward and praise him as soon as he responds correctly.

■ You can now take him safely to the local park where your dog is likely to encounter a variety of people, dogs and new situations to meet – an important lesson in socialization.

Extending leads

Use an extending lead to give some freedom of movement but do not be tempted to let him free off the lead until you can be sure he is reliable and obedient

PUPPY PLAY GROUPS

Make enquiries to see if there is a puppy play group nearby, but if you find one, do not take your puppy in until you have visited and feel that the puppies are happy and enjoying themselves. Damage can be done by any harsh treatment, or even harsh voices, at this young age. A good puppy group can be a useful experience.

TEACHING 'STAY' AND 'COME' BY USING REWARDS

1 Say 'stay', holding your hand up to reinforce the command.

2 With your hand still raised, say 'stay' and move away a little from your dog.

3 Say 'come' and repeat your dog's name. Reward him when he comes to you with your voice and a cuddle.

to the 'come' command. This may take weeks. 'Come' is all very well at home, but the distractions of the big open spaces, and other strange animals, call for a great deal of control. There is always the risk of a panic reaction to something unfamiliar. The answer is to teach 'come' on the extending lead where you can gently insist that he responds by retracting the lead; do this while you are out and about in the countryside or park. Lots of encouragement may be needed at first to face new situations, and rewards must continue for correct and immediate response. Enjoy the experience of being out with your dog as this will be transmitted to him and provide the confidence he needs.

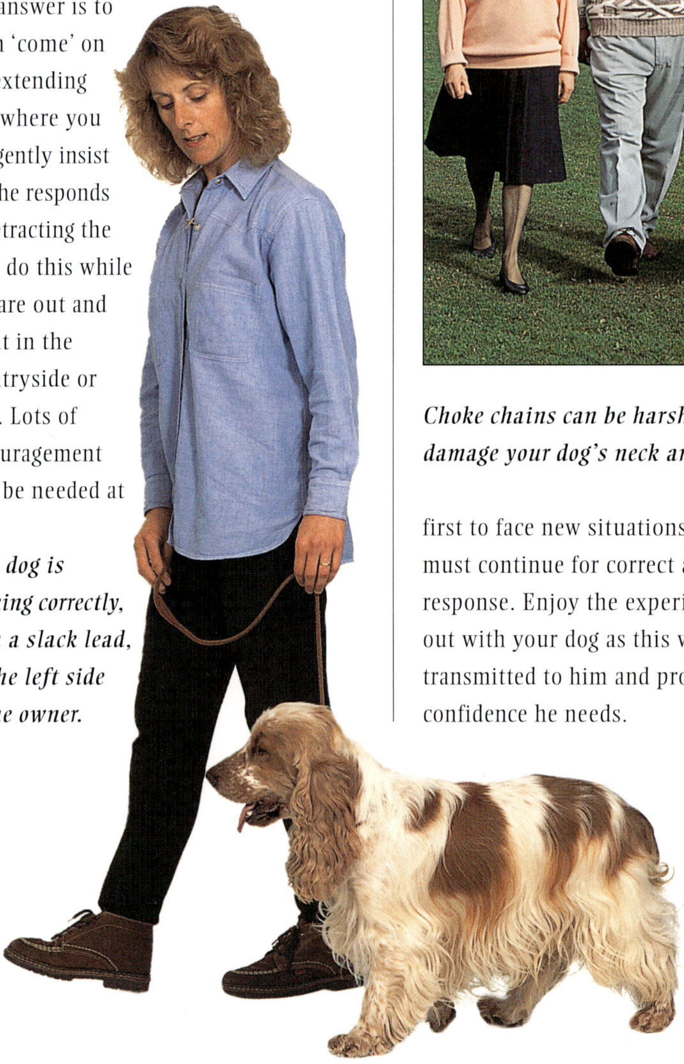

This dog is walking correctly, with a slack lead, on the left side of the owner.

Choke chains can be harsh and may damage your dog's neck and cut his coat.

PUNISHMENT

Punishment is a matter of opinion. One modern theory is that it is necessary to continually instil in the puppy the fact that you are top dog, or pack leader. You can do this, it seems, by constantly frustrating the dog so that he can see you are in command. Never allow him on your lap for a cuddle. Go and stand in his bed just when he wants to go and lie in it and tease him by picking up his feeding bowl when he is enjoying his dinner. This regime is supposed to help keep the owner as top dog and always in charge of the situation.

What is more certain is that it will lead to a dog who is wary of his owner. Dogs made to live under stressful circumstances are constantly wary and on the alert, and are sometimes the ones provoked to aggression. The basic temperament of the dog is an important factor. Some dogs are tolerant saints, putting up with the most insensitive treatment, but they shouldn't have to so so. And yet, this regime is supposed to help keep the owner as boss at all times and avoid the dog ever getting out of hand.

Some schools of training punish by hitting the dog or by shaking it by the scruff of the neck. The hitting brigade may use only rolled-up newspaper so as to frighten

Saying 'No, bad dog' is quite enough correction for most dogs.

DEVELOPING A GOOD RAPPORT

Most caring people now believe that bullying, teasing and hitting measures do nothing but destroy the trusting and affectionate relationship between man and dog. A good rapport is essential for a happy dog who enjoys game-training and wants to please. A confident dog is a happy dog, and a good cuddle and some stroking body massage at grooming time will keep him happy, not anxious, as your companion.

This does not leave the kindly trainer without the occasional sanction by way of correction. A sensitive dog is corrected easily by a change in tone of voice, and the word 'no'. The ultimate sanction is to ignore the dog for a very brief period when he wants your attention, which he will find wounding.

However, you must not resort to this punishment until you have made it perfectly clear to the dog what he has done wrong. That is, you must actually catch him in the act of disobedience or destruction, say 'no' firmly and then briefly ignore him. Use this ignoring treatment only rarely, as the final sanction.

rather than hurt. There are plenty of bullying techniques but fortunately I am not aware of any as terrible as some of the ones used in the past that caused physical injury to dogs.

Owner-dog communication

What happens so often in training a puppy, particularly if the owner has not had a dog previously, is that it is just too difficult to tune in to the world of understanding animals. It is a bit like learning a foreign language in order to try to communicate with someone who is unable to speak in reply, but who must obey your commands. It's difficult but by watching and learning from the animal, obstacles are gradually overcome and communication starts to be possible. However, where communication is slow in coming, frustration may be considerable, and this is the time when harsh methods of control may be tried. A better solution might be to forget the training if you are failing to get your message across, and simply enjoy playing with the puppy and watching his reactions until you know each other better.

Forget the training for a while, if you are failing to get your message across.

AVOIDING BAD HABITS

It is perfectly possible to avoid many of the bad habits that some dogs acquire just by applying a little common sense.

Jumping up

Dogs often show their delight at seeing you by jumping up to greet you, but many Cockers sometimes perform a different greeting ceremony. Mine bring a favourite toy to offer which avoids this problem. You may find that by providing an 'offering' toy for the dog to give you, all paws remain on the floor. If not, you can avoid the need for the dog to jump up by getting down to his level for the greeting. Or you can tell the dog to sit first, and then praise and greet him.

If you want to distract your dog from jumping up to greet you, give him a toy he can offer as a 'greeting' present.

Destructive habits

Young dogs can be very destructive, particularly during and just after the teething period. Some dogs have so little to occupy and interest them that they are destructive from sheer boredom.

The solution is to have a good play/ exercise time before going out, and then to confine the dog for a sleep in his puppy den or safe area with his toys.

SEPARATION ANXIETY

Some dogs howl miserably when left alone, causing noise nuisance to neighbours, because they are suffering the distress of separation anxiety.

Dogs are highly social pack animals and crave contact either with their own kind or with 'substitute' people. They need periods of interest and activity as well as periods of rest and sleep. Solitary confinement kills the zest for life.

When we come to think about it, we take our companion animals away from their fellow litter-mates and expect them to substitute humans for companionship. They willingly do so, but some people seem to think that they can go out for hours, sometimes even to work all day, and leave the dog alone. Like us, dogs are highly social animals and they suffer very much if left alone. For this reason, many dog breeders will not let their puppies go unless there is someone at home in the daytime. Two dogs can have more fun together than one, and provide company for each other, but this is not a solution if the owner really has insufficient time for them.

Keeping dogs shut up

- It is not difficult to imagine the intense distress of a dog, shut up alone, who maybe needs to go out for toilet purposes and in the end in desperation goes in the house. His anxiety may also lead to considerable boredom destruction.
- In this situation, on return, most

To avoid boredom, give your dog daily opportunities to run and have fun.

owners would probably punish the dog without appreciating how much the dog had suffered already. There is only one humane solution to this problem, and that is simply to arrange not to leave the dog alone for more than a couple of hours. If an emergency arises, the house is going to be empty and it is not possible to take the dog with you, exercise him well first. Then confine him to a single room with favourite safe toys. Make arrangements with a neighbour or friend to come and visit the dog and play and exercise with him in the garden.

Damage may be caused by lonely, frustrated dogs who are left alone.

■ If it is to be a long day out, it is possible to arrange for someone to come into your home to look after the dog (see useful addresses on page 144).

DOG TRAINING CLASSES

Some owners may wish to provide more formal training for their dogs by attending dog training classes. If you are planning to show your dog, ring training classes may be more appropriate and give the opportunity for further learning at the same time.

Try to find out about the range of dog training classes that are available in your area (for more information see page 144). As with puppy play groups, visit a class first without your dog to get a feeling for the atmosphere and assure yourself that this is going to be a positive and pleasant experience for your dog. Dog trainers and their teaching techniques vary a great deal.

Sometimes owners need training as well as their dogs, and in the UK a good citizen training scheme, designed to encourage basic training and responsible ownership, was introduced by the Kennel Club in 1992. Many dog training clubs run this course which provides certificates and rosettes on completion if a reasonable standard has been achieved.

CHAPTER SEVEN

GROOMING YOUR DOG

FIVE STEPS TO A WELL-GROOMED COCKER

Grooming a Cocker should be a daily routine to be enjoyed mutually by you and your dog. As a puppy, you should start the habit with a regular brushing and stroking session, preferably with the puppy standing on a table with a matt surface so that he feels secure and does not slip. By the age of six months, as the coat grows, additional attention to grooming will be needed. Be very careful

GROOMING EQUIPMENT

Although you can manage initially with just some basic grooming equipment, if you are going to cope with most of the care of a Cocker's coat yourself, you will need the following equipment: small bristle brush, pin headed brush, wide and fine toothed comb, thinning scissors and pointed end scissors, nail clippers, toothbrush and stripping comb.

not to pull any knots or tangles or the dog will soon cease to enjoy this grooming attention time.

1 The long ears of the Cocker easily become matted and any tangles should be broken up by parting carefully with your fingers. One matt quickly becomes three tiny ones and these are easily removed by using the wide-toothed comb. Comb gently down from the head to the ear tip. Keep the neck under the ear trimmed with thinning scissors. The fine hair here also becomes matted easily so keep it trimmed back to avoid problems.

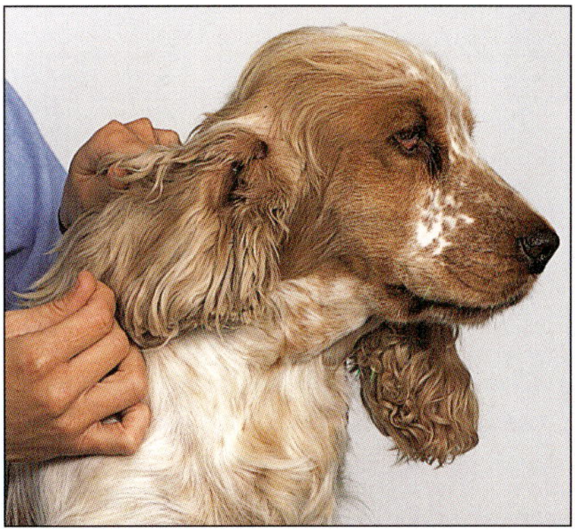

The hair under the ear should be kept short, but great care is needed to ensure that the sensitive folds of skin at the top of the ear are not nipped by the thinning scissors.

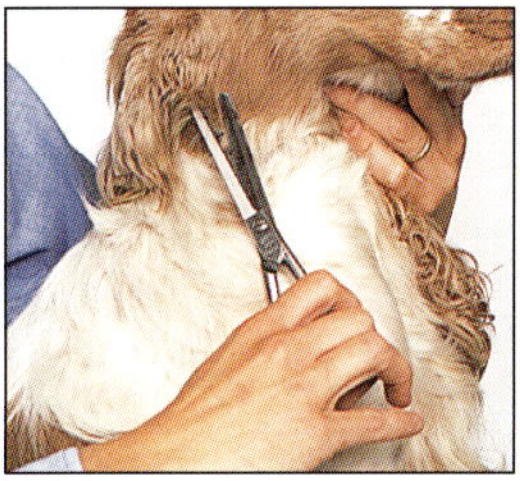

GROOMING AN UNDOCKED TAIL

You may find it easiest to groom the tail of an undocked dog by encouraging him to lie down and then brushing from the bone side of the tail downwards while the tail is spread out on the table. While he is lying down, you can use the soft brush again to brush the underhair around the tummy and under the top of the legs.

2 Next, for a treat, take the soft bristle brush and brush down the whole length of the body for several minutes to encourage a glossy shining coat. Always brush the coat in the direction you want it to lie. With a wide-toothed comb, comb the hair down the chest, down the 'trousers' under the tail and down the legs.

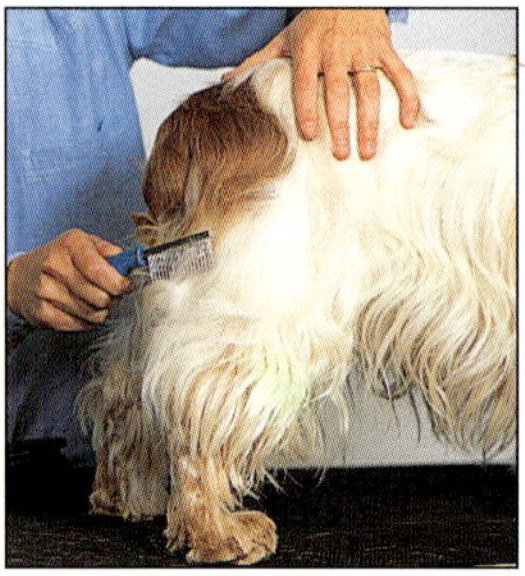

Regular brushing will keep the coat in good condition.

3 Feet should be kept neat by trimming any excess hair all round each foot and then trimming the hair between the toes. Underneath the pads, leave enough hair to afford protection.

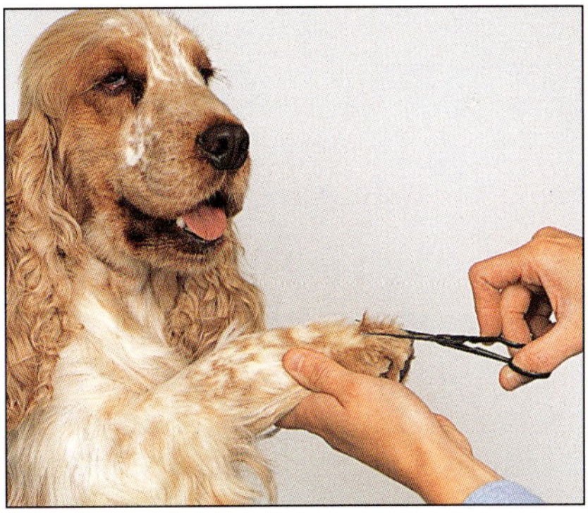

4 Finally, you may need to use a stripping knife to remove the excess whiskers on the face if they start to grow towards the eyes, but do not remove the sensor whiskers which the dog uses to test width (before he decides to try to disappear down a rabbit hole!). You will also need to use either the finger and thumb method or the stripping knife to fine down excess soft hair on the top of the head in order to give a nice smooth appearance.

PROFESSIONAL GROOMING

If you decide to seek professional grooming help, say every four months, to keep your dog in trim, look for a breeder who is willing to trim or strip a Cocker by hand. Electric clippers, so beloved by most grooming parlours, will be ruination to the natural Cocker coat and out of the question if you ever plan to show your dog. Look out for the shaven look when out and about, and contrast it with a naturally trimmed spaniel. You will see a big difference.

The dark coloured Cockers are usually more heavily coated and occasional use of a stripping knife may be justified.

5 If you want to try finger and thumb, get hold of a couple of banker's rubber finger stalls which afford an excellent grip, so that you can gently pull a little hair at a time without hurting the dog.

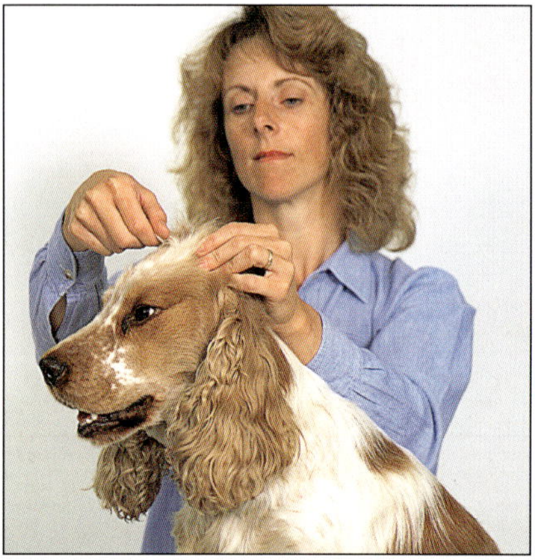

With finger and thumb, remove a very few hairs at a time from excess growth on top of the head.

Ears and mouth

Attention needs to be paid to the ears and mouth of the dog. Cotton wool buds are useful to remove any wax deposits which have worked up to the outer ear, but buds must never be pushed down into the ear.

Dental plaque can build up on the teeth but this can be reduced by using a special toothpaste for dogs available from pet stores or the vet. Used on a weekly basis, with a toothbrush at grooming time, this can be helpful in maintaining healthy teeth and gums and avoiding unpleasant breath.

Keep a regular check for build-up of ear wax and clean gently with cotton wool, avoiding poking down into the ear canal.

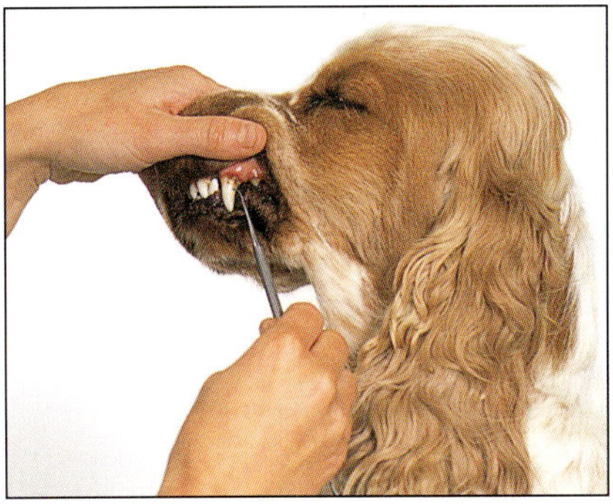

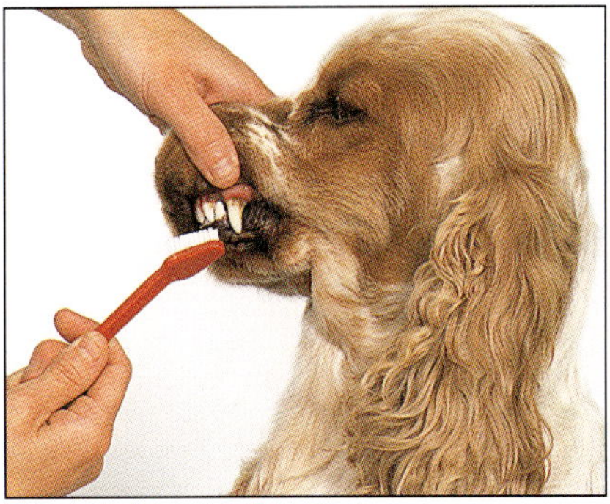

Prevent tartar forming by weekly use of a special canine toothpaste and toothbrush.

Cutting toe nails

Nail clippers need to be used at the correct angle to trim the toe nails if they appear to be growing excessively. Ask your vet, or grooming adviser, to show you how to do it for the first time. The important thing is to take off too little rather than risk too much. You have to avoid cutting the quick as this causes pain and bleeding. Light coloured nails present little problem, because you can see the quick outlined and be sure to avoid it. Black nails are more difficult so do not attempt to do them yourself if you are in any doubt.

Check your dog's eyes regularly and carefully remove any small deposits of 'sleep'.

BATHING

Once you start to bath your dog regularly, you will find it is a task that has to be continued. Dogs actually wear quite clean and their natural coats are protected in adult life by the oils that they secrete. When these oils are washed away by dog shampoo (never, please, household soap or shampoo designed for human hair) the coat is less well protected.

■ The dust and dirt from everyday life can be coped with by regular brushing as described earlier. However, if you do decide on regular bathing, you will find that your dog has a real urge to get outside as quickly as possible and have a good roll in something that smells more natural and pleasant to him. Dog shampoos are scented to please the owner, but chemical smells must cause distress to the very much greater scenting ability of the dog. As for scents sold to spray on the poor dog to make him smell nice, this is another form of unthinking human cruelty!

■ There's nothing my naughty Cockers enjoy more than finding a bit of fox's mess or another revolting scent and then rolling contentedly in it until they are well covered. It's not much fun for me if I have to drive them home in the car but I usually go prepared with those helpful zip-up towelling bags. In they go, zipped up to the neck. At one time, they might have gone straight into a bath on their return, but I've learned better now. Instead, they dry out completely and then the mess and mud brush out completely. What is more, the coat looks wonderfully shiny and the smell vanishes – an altogether happier all-round solution.

Bathing your dog

If you want to bath your dog, a plastic baby bath is a useful size to use with a non-slip rubber bath mat placed in the bottom.

1 Part-fill with warm water before lifting the dog in and soaking the coat with water from a jug. Avoid getting water into the ears. Lather the coat with a little shampoo, unscented if possible. Leave the head until last because the dog is most inclined to shake when he gets his head wet. Do not get shampoo anywhere near his eyes.

2 Rinse thoroughly to get rid of all shampoo. Lift the dog out and wrap in towels to remove most of the water. Gently dry the head and ears and dry the body and legs with further towels. Put the dog into a clean zip-up towelling bag.

This a useful investment, for use either after a bath or for travelling with a wet or dirty dog back home in the car after a country walk.

PLANNING FOR YOUR HOLIDAYS

By the time you reach this section, you will hardly have been able to avoid the conclusion that this book is written as much as possible from the dog's point of view. You won't be surprised at the suggestion that dogs deserve equal consideration when it comes to holiday plans, and the holiday the dog likes best is a holiday with you.

- **Friendly accommodation**

Not all accommodation welcomes dogs but directories and holiday guides make it clear where you can take dogs. Some hotels in the United States and Europe provide a special service and catering for dogs staying with their owners. Luxury accommodation is also available for dogs staying without owners in dog 'hotels' including comfortable rooms (not kennels!) and TV sets and music for the discriminating dog.

- **Quarantine**

Quarantine laws still exist in some countries, e.g. Great Britain. It is possible that these restrictions will be relaxed soon making it possible to holiday abroad with dogs.

- **Dog sitters**

If you can't take the dog with you, a good alternative is to have a holiday dog sitter in to look after your animals while you are away. Reputable firms send representatives to meet you first and will give you an opportunity to check on credentials. The best recommendation is to use the same sitter, or company, already tried out by someone you know. Apart from the fact that this allows animals to stay in familiar surroundings, an unwelcome break-in is less likely.

- **Boarding kennels**

Dogs accustomed to a comfortable home life are seldom happy to be shut up behind kennel bars. Before making a decision it is necessary to ask to visit boarding kennels to see the accommodation and surroundings and look at the present canine boarders, if this is permitted.

- **Infections**

The risk of picking up canine infection is increased in most kennel accommodation, particularly kennel cough, which is caused by a variety of viruses, making it difficult to protect against with a single vaccine. The stress caused to some dogs through being shut up in a strange environment can predispose them to infection.

- **Vaccinations**

Most kennels require proof of vaccination, including a recent booster inoculation, as well as protection against kennel cough.

CHAPTER EIGHT

SHOWING

ENTERING A DOG SHOW

Competitive events with dogs have never been more popular and varied than they are today. Events that permit gundogs to use their natural ability to scent, locate and retrieve are probably the most rewarding for Cockers, but opportunities for field trials are limited. Contact the Kennel Club to obtain a contact address if you wish to explore what might be available in your area (see page 144).

There are also opportunities for agility, flyball and obedience work, which are not widely supported by most Cocker owners, or ideally tuned to the keenest working

In the UK, many dog owners aim to make the show ring at Cruft's dog show. To get there, a dog must have qualified previously by having been shown at a Championship show and winning, or being placed in a class, so as to comply with current rules for qualification.

abilities of the spaniel breeds. The appeal of a well-presented show dog makes it likely that these days you will find more Cockers in the show ring than in other sporting or competitive activities.

Dog shows are held at a wide range of venues, and the enthusiast who is prepared to travel could probably find a show to attend most weeks of the year. These events are advertised regularly in the weekly dog newspapers. There is competition to gain three Challenge Certificates (or CCs) as this confers Champion or Show Champion status on the dog. It is only possible to win CCs where these are allocated for the breed at Championship shows.

Dogs and bitches are judged in separate classes at the larger shows, and classes are designated according to the age of the dog and his previous winning achievements. No puppy under six months of age can be exhibited, and there are puppy and junior classes for young dogs.

How to enter a dog show

- Entry to a show has to be made in writing to the show secretary some weeks in advance of the date of the show and entry fees paid for the classes chosen. You will be sent an entry ticket and a benching number.
- No dog can be entered for a show held under Kennel Club rules unless the dog is registered with the Kennel Club. The fun charity events with exemption dog shows are just about the only dog shows in Great Britain where unregistered dogs may be shown. ('Exemption' indicates 'exempt from normal Kennel Club rules',

There is often a more relaxed atmosphere at shows where dogs can move about in mown grass rings.

but even these shows must comply with certain Kennel Club conditions and the organisers must pay the Kennel Club for an exemption show certificate.)

■ Presentation is all important in the show dog, which means regular grooming as outlined in this book. Guidance from the breeder of your dog or a friend who shows regularly is helpful. Ringcraft classes are also most valuable in preparing a young dog for the show ring and in training the dog to stand still for the judge's inspection. Lessons in how to move with the dog on a slack lead so that the judge can assess the movement of the dog will also be given, and your dog will get used to being handled by unfamiliar people to prepare him for the judge, who will also be unknown to him.

■ The dog will be judged against the breed standard, so any dog with a serious deviation will be at a disadvantage. The judge will consider the general appearance and construction of the dog, the body shape and feel, as well as the temperament. The way the dog moves will be considered and whether that merry wagging tail is as happy as it should be.

Propping up a dog at both ends to give the judge the best impression of the dog's good points is accepted procedure.

PROCEDURE AT THE SHOW

When you arrive at the show you can ask the show secretary where Cockers are benched, or otherwise follow other Cocker exhibitors. When you have found the bench allocated to your dog, spread the benching blanket comfortably and settle your dog by attaching his benching chain through the benching ring on to your dog's collar. You will probably spend quite a lot of the day sitting on your bench with him, so you might as well make it as comfortable as you can.

Show tips

- Buy a catalogue that will show you which dogs are competing with you in the same class, and check that you and your dog are entered correctly.
- Note where the dog exercise area is allocated and make sure your dog is comfortable before he is due to go into the ring. Prepare your dog by giving a final relaxing grooming, which will set him up to show to his best advantage.
- Keep an eye on the judging so that you can note how the judge of the day prefers the dogs to move and so that you can be ready to go into the ring when your class is called. The ring steward will check your ring number, which you will need to display on your clothing by means of a ring clip. These are usually sold cheaply at dog shows, if you do not already have one.
- Your moment has come! As you enter the ring, let your dog know that you think this is enjoyable. If you are nervous and anxious, he will match your mood. You will set the dog up with correctly placed feet as the judge indicates your turn has come. Do not over-handle your dog. Set him up once as well as you can and then keep him alert and happy.
- Rosettes and prize cards may be offered for the top places. If you are out of the cards to start with, never mind. There is always another day, and another judge.
- And exhibitors who get bitten by the showing bug are seldom short of rosettes for long. Good luck!

SHOW NEEDS

- Entry ticket
- Clip to attach your ring number to your clothing
- Blanket for your dog to lie on, on his bench
- Benching chain, to secure dog to his bench
- Show lead for exhibition
- Grooming equipment
- Water and drinking bowl
- Clean-up scoop equipment

CHAPTER NINE

BREEDING

INHERITED DISEASES

Few pleasures of dog ownership are greater than watching a litter of puppies grow and develop, but before a bitch is mated, several considerations have to be taken into account, not least all the hard work of cleaning up and feeding involved until the puppies are old enough to go to their new homes. This is a full-time job!

With so many unwanted dogs being destroyed each year, only the fittest and soundest dogs should be bred from. As far as Cockers are concerned, only the happy, typical and merry dogs with first-rate reliable temperaments are suitable in a breeding plan. In addition, a check into the background for any possible inherited diseases needs to be made.

Inherited diseases

You should explain to your vet that you are considering breeding from your bitch and ask him about any inherited diseases

Puppies learn their first lessons in acceptable behaviour in the nest.

Happy, healthy Cockers are joyful companions from puppyhood to maturity and then into old age.

and the tests for inherited eye problems. Even if your bitch is perfectly healthy, she can pass serious diseases to her progeny if she carries a defective gene and is mated to a dog with a similar gene fault.

■ **Eye problems** include progressive retinal atrophy (degeneration of the retina, first noticed as night blindness), hereditary cataract (causing partial or complete blindness in one or both eyes) and entropion (the edge of the eyelid rolls inwards causing the lashes to irritate the eye).

■ **Skeletal problems** include hip dysplasia (defective hip joint causing lameness) and slipping patella (defective ligaments permitting movement of the knee cap, instead of holding it in the normal position).

■ **Familial nephropathy** is a disease of the kidneys first indicated by excessive thirst. It causes wasting and it can be diagnosed by urine tests.

By the time a bitch is old enough to be bred from, it is likely that any of these problems will have shown up, although hereditary cataract many not manifest itself until later years. It is a safeguard to tell the breeder of your bitch your plans for mating her and ask for advice on choosing a suitable stud dog for this breeding line.

MATING

Clearly a great deal of care needs to be taken in finding a possible suitable stud dog for your bitch. When you have found a dog you like, check through the points listed already at the beginning of this chapter.

It is usual to take the bitch over to the stud dog owner for the mating and when you enquire as to the dog's availability and stud fee asked, you may perhaps like to ask whether the stud owner is going to permit the dog and bitch to play together and get to know each other first so that a natural mating can hopefully ensue. The system at some kennels is to tie up the mouth of the bitch and then to hold her still throughout the proceedings and try to get her mated whether she likes the dog or not.

Although it may be most inconvenient, having made a long journey, many owners may feel that it is unwise to try to force a mating. The bitch may not be quite ready and if tried a couple of days later

TIMING AND MATING

- Bitches come into season, or on heat, roughly every six months. The first season is usually at about nine months of age. Warning signs that this is about to happen include the bitch stooping to urinate more often. She is doing what she can to give the male dogs in the area the message that she will be ready to meet them soon.
- At the very first warning, it is worth giving the bitch veterinary amplex which neutralizes odours. It is mean to spoil her fun in this way, but the fairest thing as far as you, your neighbours and local dogs are concerned. Unless you use tactics to put off the dogs in good time, you are likely to be bothered with any loose dogs that can get out to visit your premises.
- As the season progresses, the bitch's vulva will increase in size and a blood-coloured discharge will start and continue for ten to twelve days. During this time she will make a mess in the house, so she needs to be trained to lie only on her special blanket or towel. She is not ready for mating until the colour of the discharge has changed to a watery colour and the vulva has attained maximum size. At this stage, when you stroke down her back, she will switch her tail to one side in the typical manner showing she is ready for mating. You will need to keep her under close guard and surveillance and take her out in the car some distance away for exercise on a lead only throughout the three-week season.
- Regarding the best age for mating , she should be young to help ensure an easy whelping. Mating at her third season when she is about two years of age is probably ideal.

will readily submit. Alternatively, she may not like the dog and she should be allowed to reject her suitors and not be forced or frightened. Her natural instincts may be warning her that this dog will not enable her to produce the best and healthiest puppies.

You should stay with your bitch to reassure and protect her. You can always try again another day, or find another stud dog, if necessary.

The mating

- After a successful preliminary courtship, the dog will mount the bitch, clasping her with his front paws and his penis will penetrate her vulva. They will become locked together as his penis enlarges inside her and this is called the tie. It is wise to hold the collar of the bitch and dog to prevent either from pulling away from the other.
- The tie may last for about twenty minutes, or it can be anything from a few minutes to nearly an hour. When they are tied, it is usual to turn the dog so that the animals are back to back and the bitch does not have to continually support the weight of the dog.
- It is possible for a litter to be produced without a tie, but such matings seem less satisfactory. In any event, it is sensible to ask for a second mating, either the next day or in a couple of days if the bitch will still stand for the dog.

The dog and bitch should be given the opportunity to court each other so that a natural mating can follow.

Before you leave

Be sure to obtain a signed pedigree of the stud dog and a receipt for the stud fee and clear what agreement there is in the event that the bitch produces no puppies. You may be entitled to a further mating when next the bitch is in season, without further fee. Get it in writing to avoid confusion at a later date. You will also need a signed statement that the mating has taken place, in order to subsequently register the litter. The stud dog owner should be able to provide the necessary document, but these registration forms are freely available from the Kennel Club and you can obtain one in advance and make yourself familiar with the documentation needed. The dog and bitch will both need to be registered in order for the litter to qualify for full registration.

PREPARATIONS

Advise your vet of the expected whelping date. It is not easy to get a vet to attend a home whelping and often some advice and reassurance over the telephone will get the anxious owner, who is a regular client, over some problems. If there are complications it is likely that you will be asked to take the bitch over to the vet's surgery where specialist equipment is available.

Providing a whelping bed

■ You can buy purpose-made wooden whelping boxes but such equipment is not cheap, is bulky to store afterwards and should never be borrowed due to

SIGNS OF PREGNANCY

■ There are about nine weeks (sixty-three days) between the date of mating and the date when the puppies are due to be born. Owners are naturally keen to know for sure whether the bitch is in whelp or not and it is sometimes possible for a vet to tell about three weeks into pregnancy, by palpating the bitch, if puppies are present. However, time will surely tell and it may be a mistake to take her to the vet or even to ask for a scan. Bitches have the ability to spontaneously reabsorb puppies, even after they have shown up on a scan. It may be that by this means there is a reduced incidence of malformed puppies born. Despite so much man-made interference, nature still works for the best outcome, given half a chance.

■ **Drugs during pregnancy**
It may be unwise to dose the bitch with any drugs whatever during pregnancy, unless in an emergency and prescribed by the vet. De-worming treatments are best given before the bitch is mated and after the puppies are born. If you are concerned that roundworms may be present, you can arrange to have a faecal sample test, which, if clear, makes dosing unnecessary at this stage.

■ **Morning sickness**
About six weeks into pregnancy the bitch may show signs of morning sickness. At this time it is helpful to offer small meals several times a day, gradually increasing the overall daily quantity. If the litter is large, you are likely to see an increase in size of her abdomen as well as a change in her shape as the litter drops down into position in preparation for the birth.

■ **Other signs**
Seven weeks into pregnancy other signs are likely to be visible. A watery discharge from the vagina may start and there will be enlargement of the teats and mammary glands.

the difficulty of sterilizing wooden boxes and the risk of importing infection to your vulnerable new litter.

■ Stout cardboard boxes can be used provided they are of adequate size for the bitch lying outstretched. Suppliers of bulky equipment, such as TV sets, may be able to oblige if you enquire early enough. I used to get my boxes from a corrugated board manufacturer, who supplied boxes to measure with a spare supply of clean boards for the base.

■ You need to obtain the box a couple of weeks before the puppies are due and encourage the bitch to go into her new bed, made comfortable with the polyester pads.

■ How ever much trouble you take to provide a good whelping bed, she is almost certain to decide that the best and safest place to whelp is in the garden under a bush. As her time draws near, she will start to dig and as far as possible should be permitted to do so. The digging action helps with the first stage of whelping. If she is content to confine her digging to making a heap of the newspapers and pads in the whelping box, so much the better.

Just before the birth

Most bitches go off their food for a couple of days before the puppies arrive. It is as though the bitch's body is using all its reserves to prepare for the stressful event. She will become restless and may start to shiver as her temperature drops to prepare the puppies for the environmental change ahead.

She will pant intermittently and may want to go out into the garden. This is a reaction to her clean habits because she can feel that she has something inside her to pass. You will need to go with her. There is always the chance that a pup will arrive if the bitch stoops to urinate or defecate. However, if she is already having strong contractions, which you will be able to see rippling down her body as she presses downwards, the garden visit must be delayed. Reassure her by talking to her calmly.

WHELPING CHECKLIST

- Whelping box
- Washable whelping pads (polyester fleece fabric is ideal)
- Towels and rolls of kitchen paper towels
- Pig lamp or other source of adjustable heating
- Torch to keep track of bitch who will want to go outside for toilet purposes
- Glucose to add to the bitch's drinking water
- Supply of newspapers
- Scales to weigh puppies
- Emergency supply of milk powder approximating bitch's milk
- Puppy bottle feeder and sterilizing fluid

THE BIRTH

1 A dark fluid-filled bag is likely to appear first, with a gush as the fluid breaks. There is a water bag for each puppy, which sometimes breaks before the puppy arrives in its own separate sac. This sac contains amniotic fluid and the bitch will tear open the sac to enable the puppy to take its first breath. The bitch may deal out some fairly rough treatment in her efforts to lick the puppy clean and get the breathing started; but do not interfere unless she is so stunned by the arrival that she fails to make any effort to open the amniotic sac. You will then have to do so.

2 With thoroughly scrubbed hands, tear open the bag and hold the puppy, nose downwards, wiping out the mouth to remove any mucus to help the puppy breathe. Rub the pup quite briskly with clean towelling. A cry from the puppy is probably all that is needed to awaken the bitch's instincts, so that she takes over.

3 There is a placenta for each puppy to which the umbilical cord has been attached throughout pregnancy and which will arrive with or after the puppy. It is natural for the bitch to eat this as it is full of nutrients and hormones which she needs, so do not be prevent her from following her instincts.

4 The bitch will bite quite vigorously through the umbilical cord but do

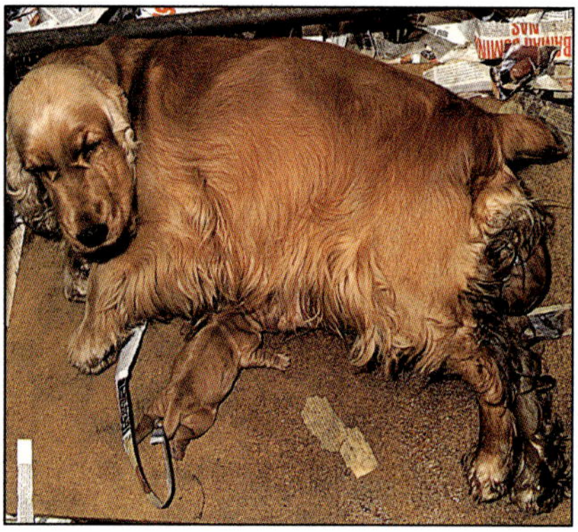

A sac containing a puppy emerges (above). The bitch tears it open (right) and licks the whelp to dry it and stimulate the first breath.

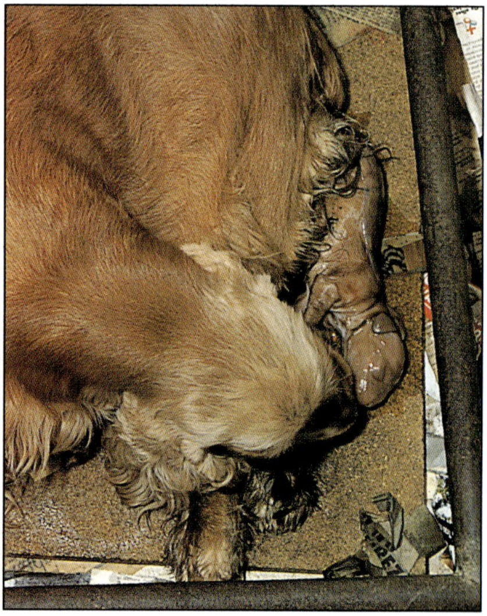

not be in too much of a hurry to do this for her if she does not do so at once. No harm will come to the pup if it remains attached to the placenta for a few minutes. If you have to step in eventually, put the fingers and thumbs of both hands on the cord about 7.5 cm (3 in) from the puppy and press the blood out of the cord and back towards the puppy. Then cut through the cord, where you have flattened it, with sterilized scissors.

5 As the whelping progresses you will find the kitchen rolls useful to mop up the copious discharge from the water bags, but keep quietly in the background if possible so as not to disturb the bitch.

6 The newly-born puppies will find their way to the teats and start to suckle before the whelping is complete. You may find that the bitch will take a drink of glucose and water, or glucose and milk, between births if the whelping is protracted.

After the delivery

After the litter has been delivered, try to encourage the bitch to leave the puppies for a minute or two to visit the garden and make herself comfortable. She will be reluctant to leave her precious babies but needs to be persuaded. She can quickly get back and settle in to the feeding and cleaning routine. Cockers make good mothers and take to their maternal duties very well.

If you alerted your vet when whelping started, make sure you report that all is well and completed afterwards. The vet may want to check the bitch and the litter the following day.

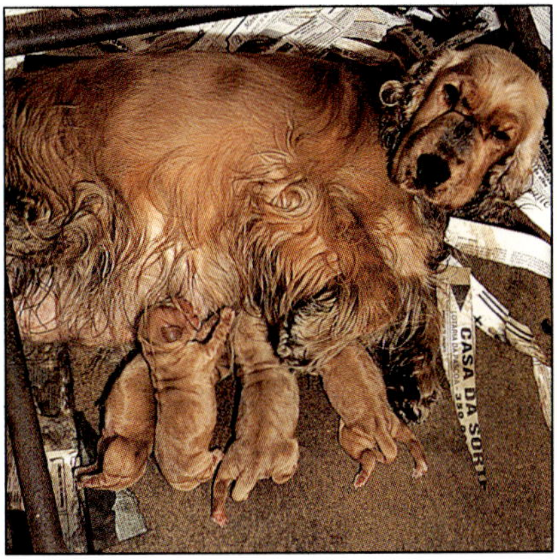

The bitch severs the cord and devours the afterbirth (left). The new-born whelps find the milk bar and feed (above).

THE FIRST FEW WEEKS

Offer the bitch an easily digested diet of scrambled eggs, chicken or boned white fish for the first few days and you may find she is still so intent and devoted to her litter that you have to hold the feeding bowl for her to ensure she eats. You should give her about five meals a day and judge the amount according to her appetite. This is one time you can feed on demand. She can gradually return to her usual diet, increasing the quantity.

Caring for the nursing bitch

The lactation period is highly demanding for the bitch because she has to take in enough food for herself and to supply her growing litter. As an approximate guide, a bitch with a litter of six puppies will need to eat three times as much as she gets in her basic daily diet, by the time the pups are three weeks of age.

■ It is important for the bitch to drink plenty of fluids to ensure a good milk supply, so make certain she takes in all the glucose and water, or glucose, milk and water, that she needs. Clean water should be available all the time.

■ Watch carefully every day to see that all the teats are being used by the puppies. If any teats show signs of becoming hard, bathe with warm/hot towelling and massage very gently to release some of the milk and try to encourage the puppies to feed from the neglected teats. Mastitis is a painful condition, if allowed to develop, and you may need to obtain antibiotics from your vet.

■ Puppies use a paddling action when they are feeding, so check the claws as they start to grow as they can become sharp quite quickly and scratch and hurt the bitch. Remove the sharp tips of the claws carefully with nail scissors.

Weaning

Weaning can start when the puppies are about four weeks of age, or a little earlier if the litter is a large one and the bitch is under pressure. Puppies should be fed individually until they have learned to feed from a bowl and to lap.

Start with a little finely scraped beef; a tiny bit can be fed from a spoon. A soaked prepared puppy diet, fed according to instructions on the pack, can then be introduced gradually.

As the pups are weaned, the bitch's milk supply will start to dry up and she must be permitted to come and go from the litter as she chooses. Shut her away from the pups for about an hour after she has been fed. In the natural state, bitches regurgitate food for their pups and she will need the nourishment herself.

PLANNING TO PART WITH THE PUPPIES

It is time to start planning to book your puppies out to good homes and prepare all the documentation. If you haven't already obtained reservations for any of the puppies you are not keeping yourself, you will need to advertise.

The useful addresses at the end of this book may assist with the last three items (below). It is possible to obtain books of insurance cover notes to enable you to issue them as each puppy leaves, and it is worth covering this vulnerable period before the puppy is fully protected from canine diseases by inoculation.

The Kennel Club registration details will be sent when you send the correct fee

YOUR NEW PUPPY OWNERS WILL NEED:

- Kennel Club certificate of litter registration
- Diet sheet showing what foods you have used for puppy feeding
- Recommended book about the breed to include grooming information (this one, hopefully!)
- Certificate of worming, or details of dates of treatment and product used
- Signed certificate of pedigree
- If you wish, insurance cover note from the moment the puppy leaves you.

and post off the document obtained and signed at the time of the mating, so do this well before the date when the puppies are due to leave you.

It is very satisfying to breed beautiful, healthy puppies and have them go to loving suitable families, but it is distressing to take back a young dog that has not settled in and has caused problems and difficulties because of lack of animal understanding. The attitude of the prospective purchaser, their lifestyle, the way in which they touch and talk to your dogs as well as a conversation about their past experience with dogs will provide a helpful guide.

Sharing this lovely breed with other appreciative people and bringing them a dog's lifetime of pleasure is a rewarding goal for any breeder.

PART THREE

HEALTHCARE

In this section on healthcare, there is expert practical advice on keeping your dog healthy and preventing many common health problems, together with information on vaccination, canine illnesses and diseases and the special health problems that may affect the breed, especially inherited ones. If you are considering breeding from your Cocker Spaniel, you will find everything that you need to know about genetically inherited diseases. Essential first-aid techniques for use in a wide range of common accidents and emergencies, including road accidents and dog fights, are also featured, with advice on when you can apply simple first-aid measures yourself, and when you should seek expert veterinary help.

HEALTH MAINTENANCE

Throughout the health section of this book, where comments relate equally to the dog or the bitch, we have used the term 'he' to avoid the repeated, clumsy use of 'he or she'. Your Cocker Spaniel is definitely not an 'it'.

SIGNS OF A HEALTHY DOG

■ Appearance and temperament

In general, a healthy dog looks healthy. He wants to play with you, as games are a very important part of a dog's life. A Cocker, being developed as a working gun dog, should always be ready for his walk, and will require a lot of exercise.

■ Eyes and nose

His eyes are bright and alert, and, apart from the small amount of 'sleep' in the inner corners, there is no discharge. His nose is usually cold and wet with no discharge, although a little clear fluid can be normal.

■ Ears

The Cocker Spaniel's ears are very sharp and responsive to sounds around him. They are long and pendulous, very hairy, and hang down over the ear canal and side of the head. The inside of his ear flap is pale pink in appearance and silky in texture. No wax will be visible and there will be no unpleasant smell. He will not scratch his ears much, or shake his head excessively.

■ Coat

A healthy Cocker Spaniel's coat will be glossy and feel pleasant to the touch. He will not scratch excessively and scurf will not be present. His coat will smell 'doggy' but not unpleasant, and he will probably shed hairs (moult) continuously, to some degree, especially if he lives indoors with the family.

■ Tail

His tail, if docked, will be about one-quarter of the full length, and the skin over the dock will be of normal thickness and will not irritate him. If left undocked, the tail will taper gradually to the tip and will be well feathered.

■ Teeth

The teeth of a healthy dog should be white and smooth. If they are yellow and dull, there may be plaque or tartar formation.

■ Claws

The claws should not be broken or too long. There is a short non-sensitive tip, as in our nails. The claws should end at the ground, level with the pad. Dogs will not pay much attention to their feet, apart from normal washing, but excessive licking can indicate disease. Cockers are born with five toes on the front feet, with one in our 'thumb' position called the dew claw, and usually four on the hind feet. Dew claws, especially on hind feet, are usually removed at three to five days of age as they become pendulous and are often injured as an adult.

■ Stools

A healthy dog will pass stools between once

POINTS OF THE COCKER SPANIEL

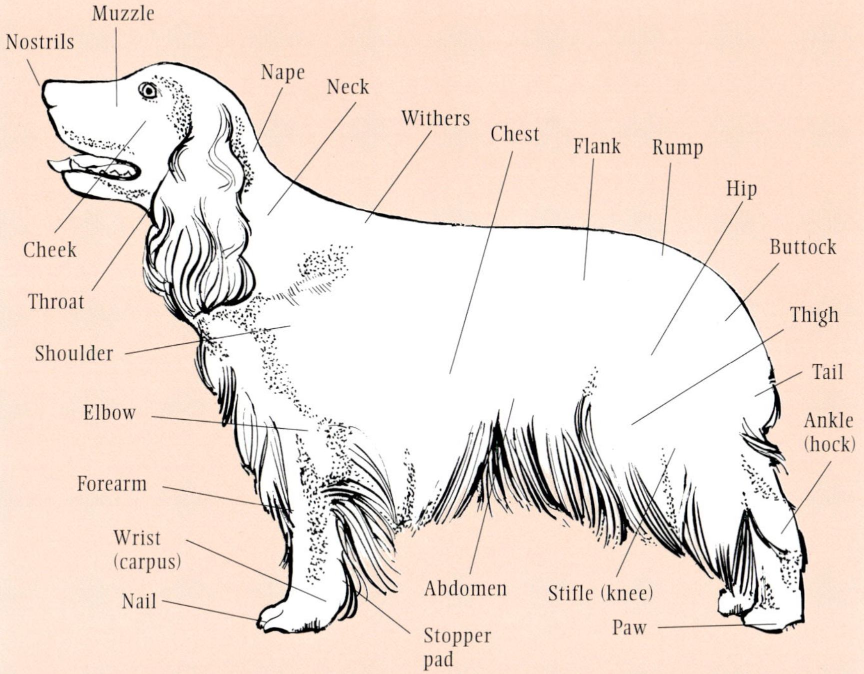

The major points of the dog are shown on the illustration above. Some of the terminology used is the same as that of the human body, but some terms may be unfamiliar, e.g. stifles (for knees) and hocks (for ankles). For an even more detailed breakdown of the parts of the dog, turn to the glossary (see page 137).

and six times a day depending on diet, temperament, breed and opportunity.

■ **Urination**

A male will urinate numerous times on a walk as this is territorial behaviour. Bitches usually urinate less often.

■ **Weight**

A healthy Cocker will look in good bodily condition – not too fat and not too thin. Sixty per cent of dogs nowadays are overweight, so you should be careful to balance your dog's diet with the right amount of exercise.

■ **Feeding**

A healthy Cocker will usually be ready for his meal and, once adult, he should be fed regularly at the same time each day. Most dogs require one meal a day, but some seem to require two meals daily just to maintain a normal weight. These are the very active dogs who tend to 'burn off' more calories.

EXAMINING YOUR DOG

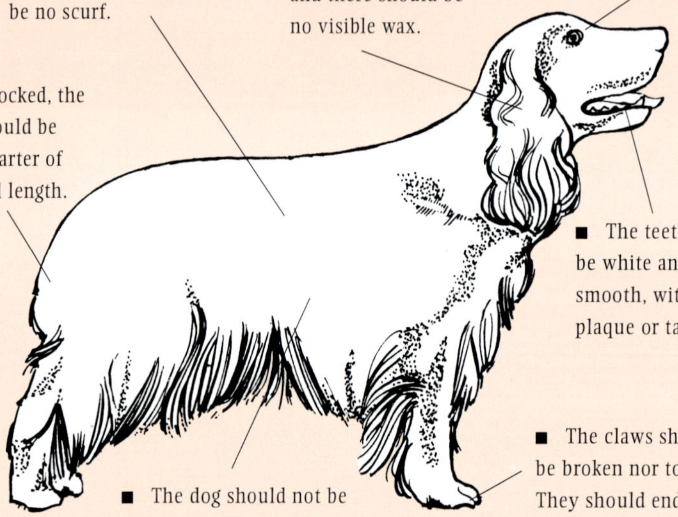

DIET

The correct diet as a puppy is essential to allow your dog to achieve his full potential during the growing phase. In a Cocker Spaniel, this is up to twelve to eighteen months of age. Many home-made diets are deficient in various ingredients just because owners do not fully appreciate the balance that is required. It is far better to rely on one of the correctly formulated and prepared commercial diets, which will contain the correct amounts and proportions of essential nutrients, such as protein, carbohydrates, fats, roughage, minerals such as calcium and phosphorus, and essential vitamins.

■ **Feeding a puppy**

Modern thinking is that the complete, dried, extruded diets that are now available have so many advantages that the new puppy could be put on to a 'growth-formula' diet of this type from as early as four weeks. Crunchy diets such as these have advantages in dental care also.

However, there are some excellent canned and semi-moist diets available, although care should be taken to check whether these are complete diets or complementary foods, which

CARE OF THE OLDER DOG

Provided that he has been well cared for throughout his life, there may be no need to treat the older Cocker Spaniel any differently as old age approaches.

■ Diet

This should be chosen to:

- ■ Improve existing problems
- ■ Slow or prevent the development of disease
- ■ Enable the dog to maintain his ideal body weight
- ■ Be highly palatable and digestible
- ■ Contain an increased amount of fatty acids, vitamins (especially A, B and E) and certain minerals, notably zinc
- ■ Contain reduced amounts of protein, phosphorus and sodium

■ Fitness and exercise

A healthy Cocker Spaniel should hardly need to reduce his exercise until he is over ten years old. There should be no sudden change in routine; a sudden increase in exercise is as wrong as a sudden drop. Let the dog tell you when he has had enough. If he lags behind, has difficulty in walking, breathing, or getting to his feet after a long walk, then it is time to consider a health check. As dogs age, they need a good diet, company, comfort and a change of scenery to add interest to their lives.

■ Avoiding obesity

As the body ages, all body systems age with it. The heart and circulation, lungs, muscles and joints are not as efficient. These should all be able to support and transport a dog of the correct weight but may fail if the dog is grossly overweight.

■ **Diet** A Cocker Spaniel of normal weight will approach old age with a greater likelihood of reaching it. It is wise to diet your dog at this stage if you have let his weight increase. Food intake can be increased almost to normal when the weight loss has been achieved.

■ **Calorie intake and nutrition** Reduce the calorie intake of your dog to about sixty per cent of normal, to encourage the conversion of body fat back into energy. Feed a high-fibre diet so that the dog does not feel hungry. Maintenance levels of essential nutrients, such as protein, vitamins and minerals, must be provided so that deficiencies do not occur.

■ **Prescription diets** Alternatively, your veterinary surgeon will be able to supply or advise on the choice of several prescription low-calorie diets, which are available in both dried and canned form, or instruct you on how to mix your own.

The dog's lifespan

Most people assume that seven years of our lives are equivalent to one year of a dog's. However, a more accurate comparison would be as follows:

- ■ 1 dog year = 15 human years
- ■ 3 dog years = 30 human years
- ■ 6 dog years = 40 human years
- ■ 9 dog years = 55 human years
- ■ 12 dog years = 65 human years
- ■ 15 dog years = 80 human years

Note: This is only an approximate guide as the larger breeds of dog tend not to live as long as the smaller breeds.

require biscuits and other ingredients to be added. If you really know your diets, it is possible to formulate a home-prepared diet from fresh ingredients.

■ A puppy should be fed four times a day until he is three months of age. A complete dried food can be left down so that he can help himself to food whenever he feels hungry. The exact amount of food given will depend on his age and the type of food, and if instructions are not included on the packet, you should consult your vet.

■ At three months of age, he should be fed three times daily, but each meal should have more in it. By six months of age, you could reduce the number of meals to two larger ones a day – still of a puppy or growth-formula food. Your puppy should remain on this type of food until he is twelve to eighteen months of age, and then change to an adult maintenance version.

■ **Feeding an adult dog**

Adult dogs can be fed on any one of the excellent range of quality dog foods now available. Your vet is the best person to advise you as to the best diet for your Cocker, and this advice will vary depending on his age, the amount of exercise he receives and his general condition.

■ **Feeding an elderly dog**

From the age of ten to twelve years onwards, your Cocker Spaniel may benefit from a change to a diet that is specially formulated for the older dog, as he will have differing requirements as his body organs age a little. Your vet is the best person with whom to discuss this, as he will be able to assess your dog's general condition and requirements.

FEEDING BOWLS

A Cocker needs a feeding bowl with deep, sloping sides to keep his ears out of the food.

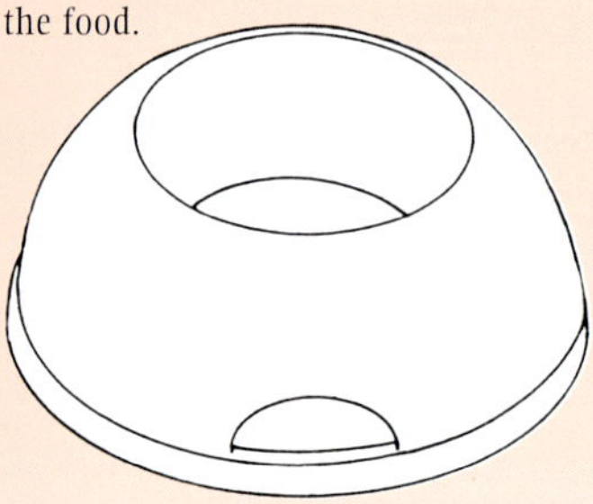

EXERCISE

As a puppy

Your Cocker Spaniel puppy should not be given too much exercise. At the age at which you acquire him, usually six to eight weeks old, he will need gentle, frequent forays into your garden, or other people's gardens provided they are not open to stray dogs. He can and should meet other vaccinated, reliable dogs or puppies and play with them. He will also enjoy energetic games with you, but remember that in any tug-of-war type contest you should win!

Although you should take your Cocker out with you to accustom him to the sights and sounds of normal life, at this stage you should not put him down on the ground in public places until the vaccination course is completed, because of the risk of infection.

About a week after his second vaccination, you will be able to take him out for walks, but remember that at this stage he is equivalent to a toddler. His bones have not calcified, his joints are still developing, and too much strenuous exercise can affect normal development. Perhaps three walks daily for about half an hour each is ample by about four

VACCINATIONS

Vaccination is the administration of a modified live, or killed, form of an infection, which does not cause illness in the dog, but instead stimulates the formation of antibodies against the disease itself.

■ **Four major diseases**
There are four major diseases against which all dogs should be vaccinated. These are as follows:

- Canine distemper (also called hardpad)
- Infectious canine hepatitis
- Leptospirosis
- Canine parvovirus

■ **Kennel cough**
Many vaccination courses now include a component against parainfluenza virus, one of the causes of kennel cough, that scourge of boarding and breeding kennels. A separate vaccine against bordetella, another cause of kennel cough, can be given in droplet form down the nose prior to your dog entering boarding kennels.
Note: All these diseases are described in Chapter Eleven (see page 107).

■ **When to vaccinate**
In the puppy, vaccination should start at eight to ten weeks of age, and consists of a course of two injections, which are administered two to four weeks apart. It is recommended that adult dogs have an annual check-up and booster inoculation by the vet.

months of age, rising to two to three hours in total by the time he reaches six months. At this stage, as his bones and joints develop, he could then be taken for more vigorous runs in the local park or the country. However, he should not be involved in really tiring exercise until he is nine months to a year old, by which time his joints have almost fully matured, and his bones have fully calcified.

As an adult dog

The exercise tolerance of an adult Cocker will be almost limitless, certainly better than most of ours! It is essential that such a lively, active, intelligent breed as the Cocker Spaniel has an adequate amount of exercise daily – it is not really sufficient to provide exercise just at weekends. A daily quota of one to two hours of interesting, energetic exercise is essential.

■ **Games during exercise** Cockers enjoy games, such as retrieving and finding hidden objects, so try to exercise your dog's brain as well as his body.

DAILY CARE

There are several things that you should be carrying out daily for your dog to keep him in first-class condition.

■ **Grooming**
All dogs benefit from a daily grooming session. Use a stiff brush or comb, which you can purchase from your vet or a pet shop, and ensure that you specify that it is for a Cocker Spaniel as brushes vary. Comb or brush in the direction in which the hair lies.

Hair is constantly growing and being shed, especially in dogs who live indoors with us, as their bodies become confused as to which season it is in a uniformly warm house. Brushing not only removes dead hair and scurf but also stimulates the sebaceous glands to produce the natural oils that keep the coat glossy and healthy.

■ **Bathing**

Dogs should not require frequent baths, but can benefit from a periodic shampoo using a specially formulated dog shampoo with a conditioner included.

■ **Feeding**

Dogs do not benefit from a frequently changed diet. Their digestive systems get used to a regular diet; dogs do not worry if they have the same food every day (that is a human trait) so establish a complete nutritious diet that your dog enjoys and stick to it.

The day's food should be given at a regular time each day. Usually the adult dog will have one meal a day, at either breakfast-time or teatime. Both are equally acceptable but, ideally, hard exercise should not be given within an hour of a full meal. It is better to give your dog a long walk and then feed him on your return. Some dogs seem to like two smaller meals a day, and this is perfectly acceptable, provided that the total amount of food given is not excessive.

■ **Water**

Your dog should have a full bowl of clean, fresh water changed once or twice a day, and this should be permanently available. This is particularly important if he is fed a complete dried food.

■ **Toileting**

Your dog should be let out into the garden first thing in the morning to toilet, and this can be taught quite easily on command and in a specified area of the garden. You should not take the dog out for a walk to toilet, unless you just do not have the space at home. The mess should be on your property and should then be picked up and flushed down the toilet daily. Other people, children in particular, should not have to put up with our dogs' mess.

■ Throughout the day, your dog should

TEETH AND JAWS

The molars crush the food whereas the incisors (smaller front teeth) are used for scraping. The large, pointed canine teeth are used for tearing meat.

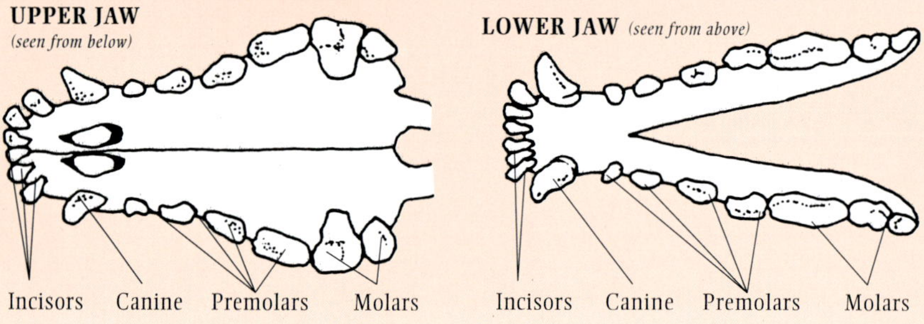

have access to a toileting area every few hours, and always last thing at night before you all go to bed.

■ Dogs will usually want to, and can be conditioned to, defecate immediately after a meal, so this should be encouraged.

■ **Company**

Cockers are very sociable dogs and bond to you strongly. There is no point in having one unless you intend to be there most of the time. Obviously, a well-trained and socialized adult should be capable of being left for one to three hours at a time, but puppies need constant attention if they are to grow up well balanced. Games, as mentioned before, are an essential daily pastime.

■ **Dental care**

Some complete diets are very crunchy, and by mimicking the diet of wild dogs, e.g. foxes and wolves, of a whole rabbit (bones, fur etc.), they can keep your dog's teeth relatively free of plaque and tartar. However, a daily teeth inspection is sensible. Lift the lips and look not only at the front incisor and canine teeth but also at the back premolars and molars. They should be a healthy, shiny white, just like ours.

■ **Cleaning teeth**

If not, or if on a soft, canned or fresh meat diet, daily brushing with a toothbrush and enzyme toothpaste is advisable. Hide chew sticks help clean teeth, as do root vegetables, such as carrots, and many vets recommend a large raw marrow bone. These can, however, occasionally cause teeth to break. Various manufacturers have brought out tasty, chewy food items that benefit teeth, and your vet will be able to recommend a suitable one.

■ **Temporary teeth**

Pups are born with, or acquire shortly after birth, a full set of temporary teeth. These start to be shed at about sixteen weeks of age with the central incisors, and the transition from temporary to permanent teeth should be complete by the time they are six months old. If extra teeth seem to be present, or if teeth seem out of position at this age, it is wise to see your vet.

GENERAL INSPECTION

A full inspection of your dog is not necessary on a daily basis, unless you notice something different about him. However, it is as well to cast your eyes over him to ensure that:

- The coat and skin are in good order
- The eyes are bright
- The ears are clean
- The dog is not lame

Check that he has eaten his food, and that his stools and urine look normal.

PERIODIC HEALTH CARE

Worming

■ **Roundworms (Toxocara)**

All puppies should be wormed fortnightly from two weeks to three months of age, and then monthly until they are six months old. Thereafter in a male or neutered female Cocker, you should worm twice yearly. Bitches used for breeding have special roundworming requirements and you should consult your vet about this. There is evidence that entire females undergoing false (pseudo) pregnancies have roundworm larvae migrating in their tissues, so they should be wormed at this time.

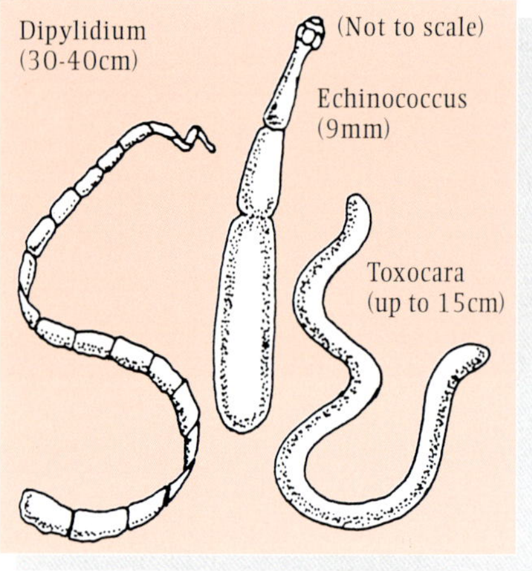

■ **Tapeworms (Dipylidium and Echinococcus)**
These need intermediate hosts (fleas and usually sheep offal respectively) to complete their life cycle, so prevention of contact with these is advisable. As a precaution, most vets recommend that you should tapeworm adult dogs twice a year.

WORMING YOUR DOG

Dogs need to be wormed regularly for roundworms:

- Fortnightly for puppies from two weeks to three months of age
- Monthly for puppies from three months to six months of age
- Twice yearly thereafter in male dogs and neutered females

Note: Bitches used for breeding have special requirements – ask your vet. Adult dogs should be wormed twice a year for tapeworms.

■ **Treatment** There are very effective and safe combined round wormers and tape worm treatments available now from your vet.

SPECIAL HEALTH PROBLEMS

The Cocker Spaniel is usually a fit, friendly and interesting companion. However, there are some health problems that are known to occur in this breed particularly. A few of the most common problems are detailed below.

■ **Progressive retinal atrophy (PRA)**
This is an inherited progressive degeneration of the retina of the eye, found in the Cocker and other breeds, which may lead to total blindness. Affected dogs of either sex must not be used for breeding. This disease is covered more fully in Chapter Eleven under eye diseases (see page 117).

■ **Entropion**
This is an inherited disease, usually of the young, growing dog, which is seen quite often in the Cocker. The edge of an eyelid rolls inwards so that the lashes rub against the surface of the eye, causing irritation of the eyeball. The eye is sore and wet with tears, and often kept closed. Surgical treatment is necessary.

■ **Persistent pupillary membrane**
As the name suggests, this is a band of tissue attached to the iris which affects vision. It is inherited in the Cocker.

■ **Familial nephropathy**
This is an inherited disease which is seen in the Cocker, whereby the kidneys fail at an early age, resulting in death. Unfortunately, there is no treatment.

■ **Glaucoma**
An inherited disease in Cockers, glaucoma develops when the pressure of the fluid inside the eye increases, causing the dog pain, inflammation and excessive tear production.

■ **Ectropion**

Also inherited, this disease is the opposite to entropion; the eyelid rolls outwards instead of inwards.

INHERITED EYE DISEASES

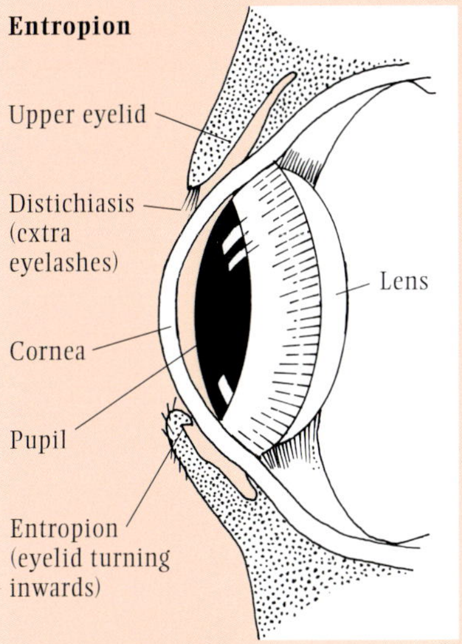

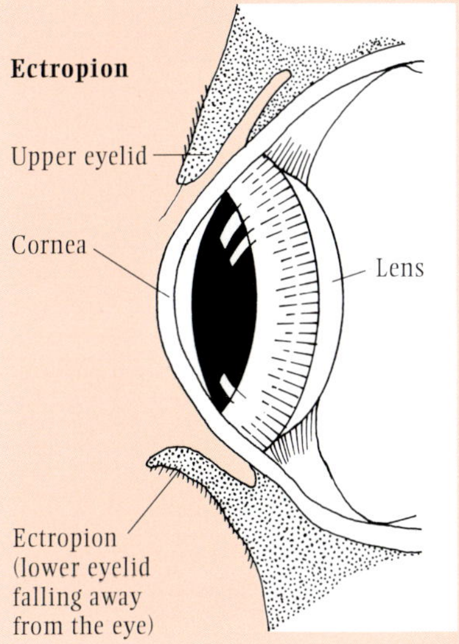

■ **Distichiasis**

This is an inherited defect of the Cocker Spaniel in which fine extra hairs grow along the edge of the eyelid and rub against the cornea of the dog.

■ **von Willebrand's disease**

This is an inherited disease of a blood component, the platelets, and causes haemorrhage. The Cocker Spaniel is one of the breeds in which it is known to be inherited.

Note: in addition to the specific advice given above, you can reduce the chances of your new dog having these problems by asking the right questions about his ancestry before you purchase him. Apart from entropion, familial nephropathy and PRA, all the above problems are uncommon.

PET HEALTH INSURANCE

By choosing wisely in the beginning, and then ensuring that your dog is fit, the right weight, occupied both mentally and physically, protected against disease by vaccination, and fed correctly, you should be able to minimize any vet's bills. The unexpected may well happen though. Accidents and injuries occur, and dogs can develop lifelong allergies or long-term illnesses, such as diabetes. Pet health insurance is available and is recommended by the vast majority of veterinarians for such unexpected eventualities. It is important to take out a policy that will suit you and your Cocker Spaniel, so it is wise to ask your veterinary surgeon in advance for his recommendation.

11

DISEASES AND ILLNESSES

RESPIRATORY DISEASES

■ Rhinitis

An infection of the nose caused by viruses, bacteria or fungi, this occurs in the Cocker Spaniel but is not very common. It may also be part of a disease such as distemper or kennel cough. Sneezing or a clear or coloured discharge are the usual signs.

Another cause, due to the dog's habit of sniffing, is a grass seed or other foreign object inhaled through the nostrils. The dog starts to sneeze violently, often after a walk through long grass.

■ Tumours of the nose

These are also seen occasionally in the Cocker Spaniel. The first sign is often haemorrhage from one nostril. X-rays reveal a mass in the nasal chamber.

Diseases producing a cough

A cough is a reflex which clears foreign matter from the bronchi, trachea and larynx. Severe inflammation of these structures will also stimulate the cough reflex.

■ Laryngitis, tracheitis and bronchitis

Inflammation of these structures can be

THE RESPIRATORY SYSTEM

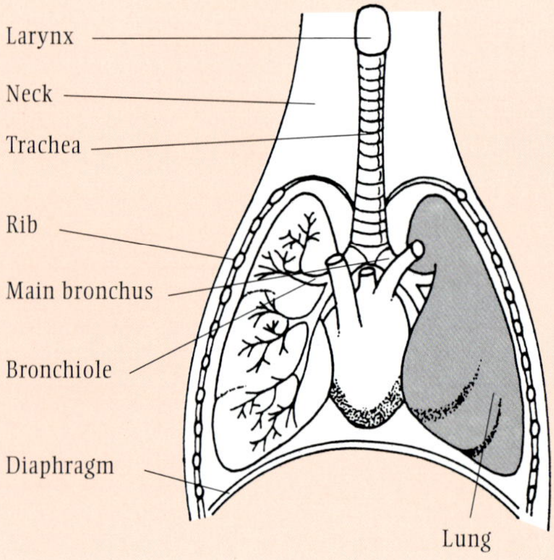

The larynx, trachea, lungs and bronchi, together with the nose, make up the dog's respiratory system. Air is inhaled through the nose, filtered and passed through the larynx into the trachea. It enters the lungs through the bronchi, which subdivide into bronchioles and end in alveoli, or air sacs. Oxygen and carbon dioxide gases are exchanged in the alveoli.

INFECTIOUS DISEASES

■ **Distemper (hardpad)**
This is a frequently fatal virus disease which usually affects dogs under one year of age. Affected dogs cough and have a discharge from the eyes and nose. Pneumonia often develops, and vomiting and diarrhoea usually follow. If the dog lives, nervous symptoms, such as fits, paralysis or chorea (a type of regular twitch), are likely. The pads of the feet become thickened and hard and hence the other name for the disease – hardpad.

■ **Treatment** by antibiotics sometimes helps, but the only real answer is prevention by vaccination as a puppy, and annual boosters thereafter.

■ **Infectious canine hepatitis**
This disease affects the liver. In severe cases, the first sign may be a dog going off his food completely and becoming very depressed and collapsed. Some dogs die suddenly. Recovery is unlikely from this severe form of the disease. Prevention by vaccination is essential.

■ **Leptospirosis**
Two separate diseases can affect dogs. Both, in addition to causing severe and often fatal disease in the dog, are infectious to humans.

■ **Leptospira canicola** causes acute kidney disease.

■ **Leptospira icterohaemorrhagiae** causes an acute infection of the liver, often leading to jaundice.

■ **Treatment** of both diseases is often unsuccessful, and prevention by vaccination is essential.

■ **Canine parvovirus**
This disease affects the bowels, causing a sudden onset of vomiting and diarrhoea, often with blood, and severe depression. As death is usually due to dehydration, prompt replacement of the fluid and electrolyte loss is essential. In addition, antibiotics are usually given to prevent secondary bacterial infection. Prevention by vaccination is essential.

■ **Kennel cough**
This is a highly infectious cough, which occurs principally in kennelled dogs. There are two main causes:

■ Bordetella, a bacterial infection
■ Parainfluenza virus

Both affect the trachea and lungs. Occasionally, a purulent discharge from the nose and eyes may develop. Antibiotics and rest are usually prescribed by the vet. Prevention of both by vaccination is recommended.

caused by infection, such as kennel cough or canine distemper, by irritant fumes or by foreign material. Usually, all three parts of the airway are affected at the same time.

Bronchitis is a major problem in the older dog and is caused by a persistent infection or irritation, producing irreversible changes in the bronchi. A cough develops and increases until the dog seems to cough almost constantly.

Diseases producing laboured breathing

Laboured breathing is normally caused by those diseases which occupy space within the chest, and reduce the lung tissue available for oxygenation of the blood. An X-ray produces an accurate diagnosis.

- **Pneumonia**

This is an infection of the lungs caused by:

- Viruses
- Bacteria
- Fungi or inhaled matter, such as water

- **Chest tumours**

These can cause respiratory problems by occupying lung space and by causing the accumulation of fluid within the chest.

Accidents

Respiratory failure commonly follows accidents. Several types of injury may be seen in dogs:

- **Haemorrhage into the lung**

Rupture of a blood vessel in the lung will release blood which fills the air sacs.

- **Ruptured diaphragm**

This allows abdominal organs, such as the liver, spleen or stomach, to move forwards into the chest cavity.

HEART AND CIRCULATION DISEASES

Heart attack in the human sense is uncommon. Collapse or fainting may occur due to inadequate cardiac function.

Heart murmurs

- **Acquired disease**

This may result from wear and tear or from inflammation of heart valves, problems of rhythm and rate, or disease of the heart muscle. Signs of disease may include:

- Weakness
- Lethargy

SECTION OF THE HEART

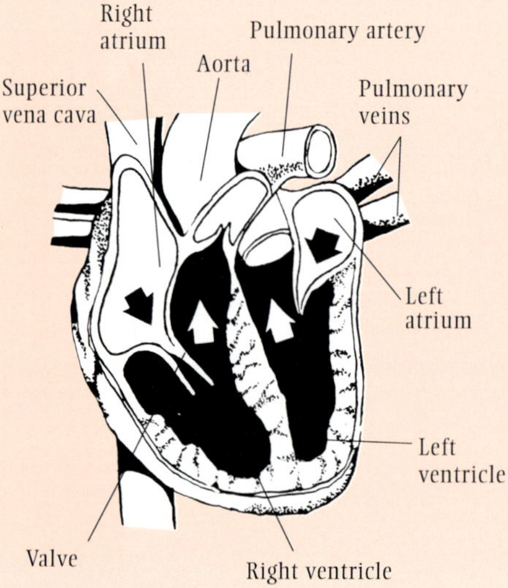

The heart consists of two pairs of chambers: the atria and the ventricles. Deoxygenated blood enters the right atrium and is pumped out through the right ventricle to the lungs where it is oxygenated. This blood flows into the left atrium and thence through the left ventricle to the body's organs.

THE CIRCULATORY SYSTEM

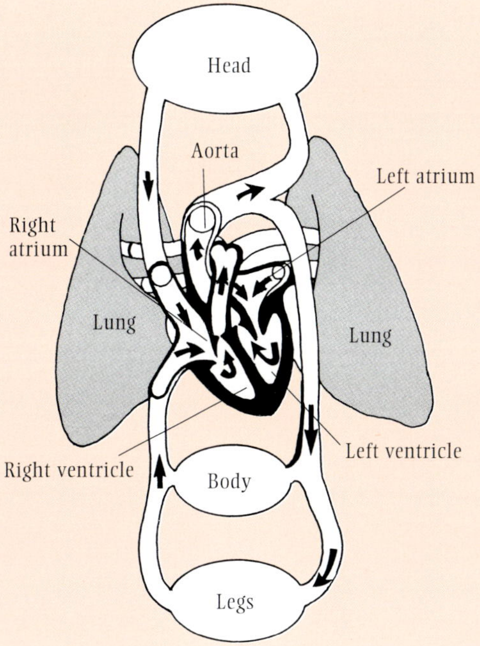

Blood circulates around the dog's body by way of the circulatory system.

- Oxygenated blood is pumped by the heart through the arteries to all the body organs, e.g. the brain, muscles and liver.
- Oxygen and nutrients are extracted from the blood.
- The used blood is returned by the veins to the right ventricle and then to the lungs.
- In the lungs, carbon dioxide is exchanged for oxygen.

- Panting
- Cough
- Abdominal distension
- Collapse
- Weight loss

Congenital heart disease

This is usually due to valve defects or a hole in the heart. Both are seen fairly frequently in the Cocker Spaniel. Signs of disease may include:

- Weakness and failure to thrive or grow at a normal rate
- The sudden death of a puppy

Note: congestive heart failure is the end result of any of these defects.

SIGNS OF HEART FAILURE

These may include the following:

- Exercise intolerance
- Lethargy
- Panting and/or cough
- Enlargement of the abdomen due to fluid accumulation
- Poor digestion and weight loss

Veterinary investigation involves thorough examination, possibly X-rays of the chest, ECG, and, in some cases, ultrasound scanning.

Heart block

This is an acquired problem. A nerve impulse conduction failure occurs in the specialized heart muscle, which is responsible for maintaining normal rhythm and rate.

Blood clotting defects

■ **Clotting problems**
These may result from poisoning with Warfarin rat poison. Haemorrhage then occurs which requires immediate treatment (see first aid, page 129).

■ **Congenital clotting defects**
These arise if the pup is born with abnormal blood platelets or clotting factors, both of which are essential in normal clotting. Von Willebrand's disease is an inherited clotting disorder sometimes found in Cocker Spaniels.

Tumours

The spleen, which is a reservoir for blood, is a relatively common site for tumours, especially in older dogs. Splenic tumours can bleed slowly into the abdomen or rupture suddenly, causing collapse. Surgical removal of the spleen is necessary.

DIGESTIVE SYSTEM DISEASES

Mouth problems

Dental disease

■ **Dental tartar** This forms on the tooth surfaces when left-over food (plaque) solidifies on the teeth. This irritates the adjacent gum, causing pain, mouth odour, gum recession and, ultimately, tooth loss. The inevitable progression to periodontal disease may be prevented if plaque is removed by regular tooth brushing coupled with good diet, large chews and hard biscuits.

■ **Periodontal disease,** or inflammation and erosion of the gums around the tooth roots, is very common. It is a particularly common problem of the Cocker Spaniel, probably because of saliva accumulation due to the lip folds. Careful scaling and polishing of the teeth by your vet under an anaesthetic is necessary to save the teeth.

■ **Dental caries** (tooth decay) is common in people, but not so in dogs, *unless they are given chocolate or other sweet foods.*

■ **Tooth fractures** can result from trauma in road accidents or if your dog is an enthusiastic stone catcher or chewer. A root treatment may be needed.

■ **Epulis** is a benign overgrowth of the gum. Surgical removal is needed.

Salivary cysts

These may occur as soft, fluid-filled swellings under the tongue or neck, resulting from a ruptured salivary duct.

Mouth tumours

These are often highly malignant, growing rapidly and spreading to other organs. First symptoms may be bad breath, increased salivation, and bleeding from the mouth plus difficulties in eating.

■ **Foreign bodies in the mouth**
(See first aid, page 134)

Problems causing vomiting

■ **Gastritis**
This is inflammation of the stomach and can

THE DIGESTIVE SYSTEM

The mouth, throat, oesophagus, stomach, intestines, liver and pancreas together make up the digestive system. When food is swallowed, it passes through the oesophagus into the stomach and intestines where it is broken down by enzymes. Nutrients are absorbed by the body, and waste matter is eliminated via the rectum.

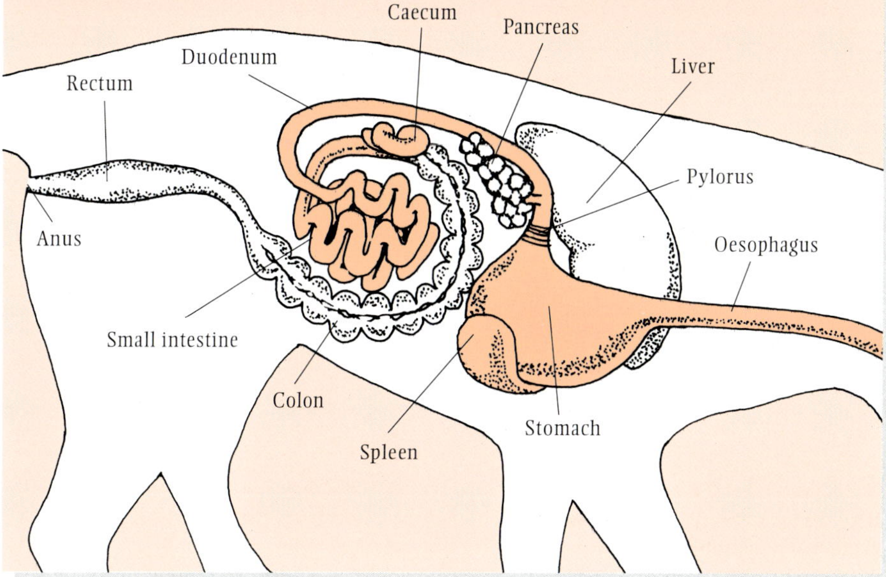

result from unsuitable diet, scavenging or infection. The dog repeatedly vomits either food or yellowish fluid and froth, which may be blood stained.

■ **Obstruction of the oesophagus**
This leads to regurgitation of food immediately after feeding, and may be caused by small bones or other foreign bodies. Diagnosis is confirmed by X-ray or examination with an endoscope and treatment must not be delayed.

■ **Megoesophagus**
This is a defect in the wall of the oesophagus due to faulty nerve control, which leads to ballooning, retention of swallowed food and regurgitation before the food reaches the stomach.

■ **Obstruction lower down the gut, in the stomach or intestine**
This may result from items such as stones, corks etc. Tumours can also lead to obstructive vomiting. The dog rapidly becomes very ill and the diagnosis is usually confirmed by palpation, X-rays or exploratory surgery.

■ **Intussusception**
This is telescoping of the bowel which can

PROBLEMS CAUSING DIARRHOEA

- **Dietary diarrhoea**

This can occur as a result of sudden changes in diet, scavenging, feeding unsuitable foods or stress (especially in pups when they go to their new home).

- **Pancreatic insufficiency**

(See below)

- **Enteritis**

This is an inflammation of the small intestine which can be caused by infection, e.g. parvovirus, a severe worm burden or food poisoning. Continued diarrhoea leads to dehydration.

- **Colitis**

This is inflammation of the large bowel (colon), and symptoms include straining and frequent defecation, watery faeces with mucous or blood, and often an otherwise healthy dog.

- **Tumours of the bowel**

Tumours of the bowel are more likely to cause vomiting than diarrhoea, but one called lymphosarcoma causes diffuse thickening of the gut lining which may lead to diarrhoea.

follow diarrhoea, especially in puppies. Surgery is essential.

- **Gastric dilatation**

(See first aid, page 135)

Pancreatic diseases

- **Acute pancreatitis**

This is an extremely painful and serious condition requiring intensive therapy. It can be life-threatening.

- **Pancreatic insufficiency**

Wasting of the cells of the pancreas which produce digestive enzymes leads to poor digestive function, persistent diarrhoea, weight loss and ravenous appetite. The condition, when it occurs, is often diagnosed in dogs of less than two years of age, and is occasionally seen in the Cocker Spaniel. Diagnosis is made on clinical symptoms and laboratory testing of blood and faeces.

- **Diabetes mellitus (sugar diabetes)**

Another function of the pancreas is to manufacture the hormone insulin, which controls blood sugar levels. If insulin is deficient, blood and urine glucose levels rise, both of which can be detected on laboratory testing. Affected animals have an increased appetite and thirst, weight loss and lethargy. If left untreated, the dog may go into a diabetic coma.

- **Pancreatic tumours**

These are relatively common and are usually highly malignant. Symptoms vary from vomiting, weight loss and signs of abdominal pain to acute jaundice. The prognosis is usually hopeless, and death rapidly occurs.

LIVER DISEASES

- **Acute hepatitis, infectious canine hepatitis and leptospirosis**

For more information, see infectious diseases (page 107). These diseases are not common as most dogs are vaccinated.

- **Chronic liver failure**

This can be due to heart failure, tumours or cirrhosis. Affected dogs usually lose weight and become depressed, go off their food and may vomit. Diarrhoea and increased thirst are other possible symptoms. The liver may increase or decrease in size, and there is sometimes fluid retention in the abdomen. Jaundice is sometimes apparent. Diagnosis of liver disease depends on symptoms, blood tests, X-rays or ultrasound examination, and possibly liver biopsy.

SKIN DISEASES

Itchy skin diseases

Parasites

■ **Fleas** These are the commonest cause of skin disease, and dogs often become allergic to them. They are dark, fast-moving, sideways-flattened insects, about two millimetres long.

STRUCTURE OF THE SKIN

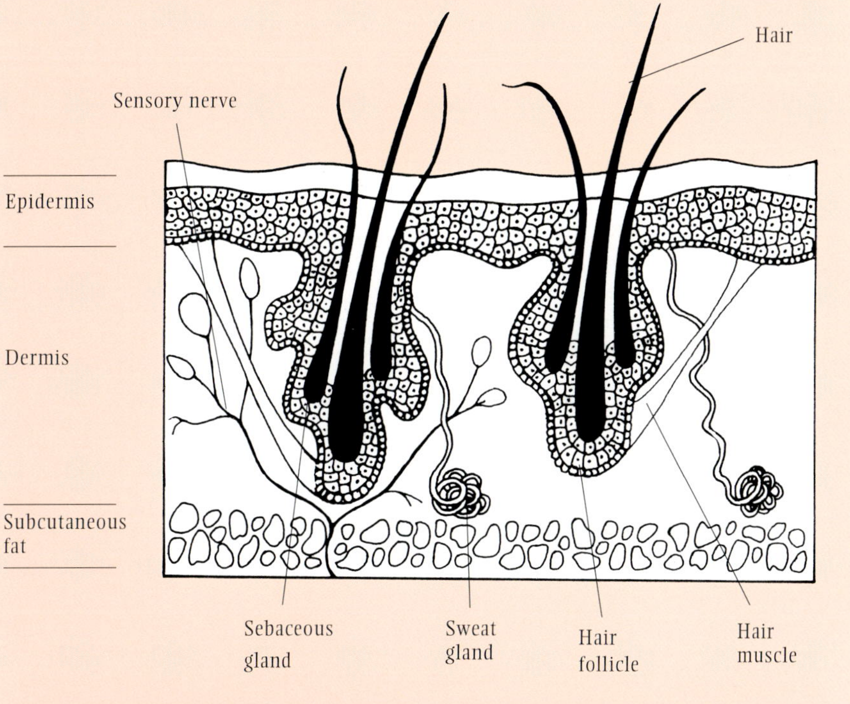

The epidermis (the tough, outer layer of skin) consists of dead cells which are constantly wearing away on the surface and being replaced with new ones from underneath. The underlying dermis is a thicker layer, containing hair follicles, sweat glands and blood vessels. Below this is an insulating layer of subcutaneous fat.

PARASITES

(Not to scale)

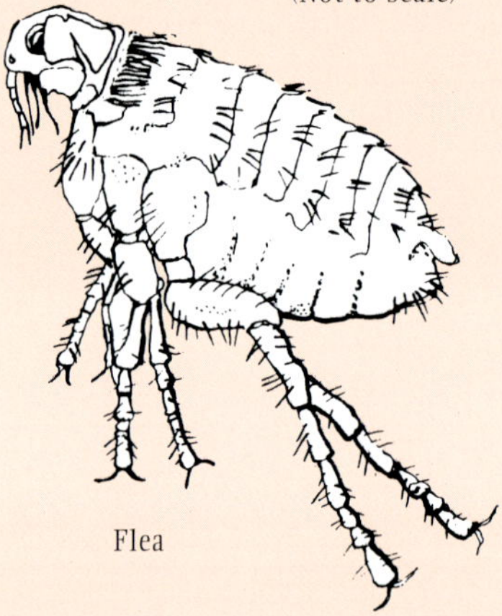

Flea

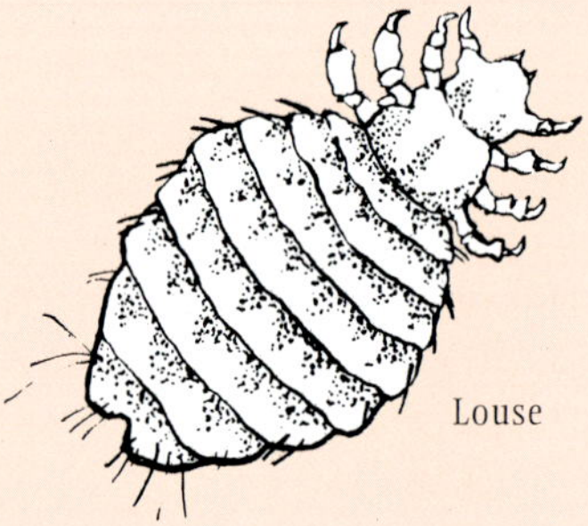

Louse

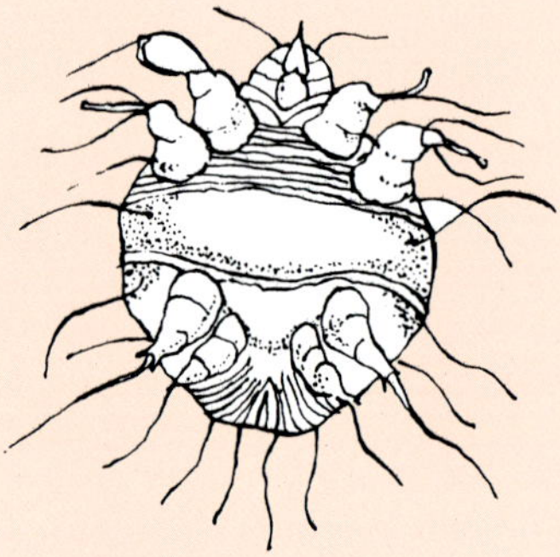

Sarcoptic mite

They spend about two hours a day feeding on the dog, then jump off and spend the rest of the day breeding and laying eggs. They live for about three weeks and can lay fifty eggs a day. Thus each flea may leave behind 1,000 eggs which hatch out in as little as three weeks. It is important to treat the dog with an effective, modern veterinary product, and also the environment, i.e. the dog's basket and bedding and other areas in the house. Ask your vet for advice on which are the best products to use, e.g. sprays, washes or powders.

■ **Lice** are less common, but seem to enjoy life on spaniels' long, floppy ears. They are small, whitish insects crawling very slowly between and up the hairs. They lay eggs on the hair, spend their entire life on the dog and are much easier to treat than fleas. Again, ask you vet to recommend a suitable parasiticidal preparation for killing lice.

■ **Mange** is caused by mites (usually Sarcoptes) which burrow into the skin, causing intense irritation and hair loss. It is very contagious and more common in young dogs. Treatment is by anti-parasitic washes.

■ **Bacterial infections**

These are common in the dog and are often secondary to some other skin disease, such as mange or allergies. Long-term antibiotics are needed to control some skin diseases.

■ **Pyoderma**

This can be an acute, wet, painful area of the skin (wet eczema), or a more persistent infection appearing as ring-like sores. Both are quite common in the Cocker Spaniel.

■ **Furunculosis**

This is a deeper, more serious infection which is seen quite often in the Cocker Spaniel.

■ **Contact dermatitis**

This is an itchy reddening of the skin, usually of the abdomen, groin, armpit or feet, where the hair is thinnest and less protective. It can be an allergic response to materials, such as wool, nylon or carpets, or to a direct irritant, such as oil, or a disinfectant.

■ **Lick granuloma**
This is a thickened, hairless patch of skin, usually seen on the front of the wrist or the side of the ankle. It is seen in the Cocker and is thought to result from constant licking of this area because of boredom or neurosis.

■ **Atopy** This itchy allergic skin disease is due to inhaled allergens.

Non-itchy skin diseases

■ **Demodectic mange**
Caused by a congenitally-transmitted parasitic mite, usually in growing dogs, and causes non-itchy patchy hair loss. It is difficult to treat.

■ **Ticks**
These are parasitic spiders resembling small grey peas that attach themselves to the skin. They drop off after a week, but should be removed when noticed. Soak them with surgical spirit and pull them out using fine tweezers.

Tick

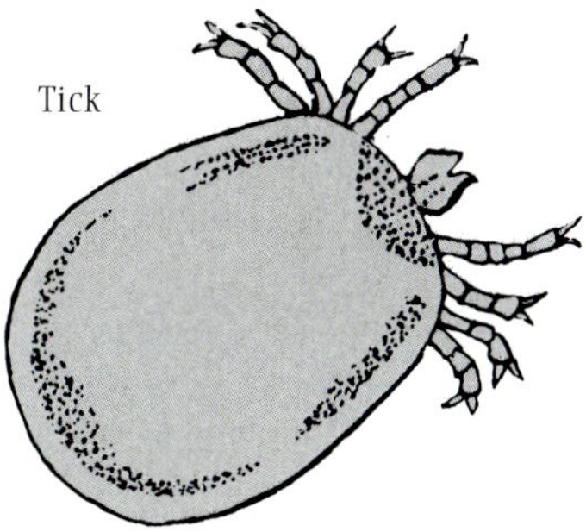

■ **Ringworm**
This is a fungal infection of the hairs and skin causing bald patches. It is transmissible to people, especially children. Always wear rubber gloves when handling a dog with ringworm. Any infected hair should be removed and the skin cleansed with a fungicidal wash. Consult your vet for advice.

■ **Hormonal skin disease**
This patchy, symmetrical hair loss is not common in the Cocker Spaniel, but spayed female Cockers invariably develop a fluffy soft coat after their operation.

TUMOURS AND CYSTS

■ **Sebaceous cysts**
These are round, painless nodules in the skin and vary from 2 mm up to 4 cm in diameter. They are seen in Cocker Spaniels, particularly as they get older.

■ **Warts**
These are very common in the older Cocker Spaniel, and often develop in large numbers. Other skin tumours do occur.

■ **Anal adenomas**
These frequently develop around the anus in old male dogs. They ulcerate when they are quite small and produce small bleeding points.

DISEASES OF THE ANAL AREA

Anal sac impaction
This is quite common in the Cocker Spaniel, and is thought by some authorities to be linked with the tradition of docking the tail. The anal sacs are scent glands and little used in the dog. If the secretion accumulates in the gland instead of being emptied during defecation as the dog raises his tail, the over-full anal sac become itchy. The dog drags his anus along the ground or bites himself around the base of his tail. Unless the sacs are emptied by your vet, an abscess may form.

STRUCTURE OF THE FOOT

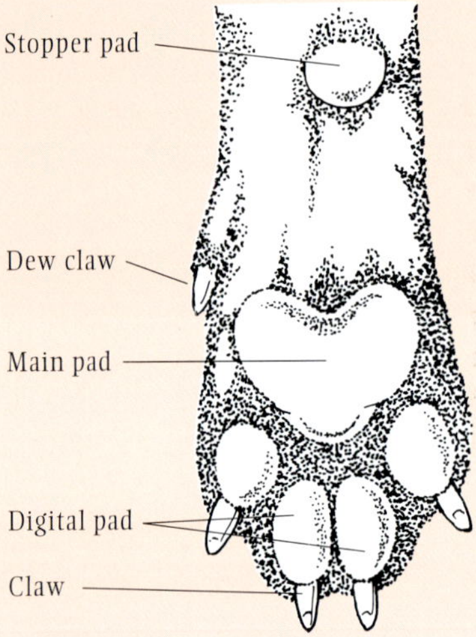

DISEASES OF THE FEET

■ **Interdigital eczema**
Cockers readily lick their feet after minor damage, and this makes the feet very wet. Infection then occurs between the pads.

■ **Interdigital cysts and abscesses**
These are painful swellings between the toes which may make the dog lame. In most cases the cause is unknown, but in hairy-footed dogs like Cocker Spaniels, they can be caused by a grass seed penetrating the skin between the toes.

■ **Foreign body in the pad**
The most common foreign body to become lodged in the pads is a sharp fragment of glass, or a thorn. The dog is usually very lame and the affected pad is painful to the touch. Often an entry point will be seen on the pad.

■ **Nail bed infections**
The toe becomes swollen and painful and the dog becomes lame. The bone may become diseased and this can lead to amputation of the affected toe.

EAR DISEASES

Haematoma

Painless, sometimes large, blood blisters in the ear flap, haematomas are usually caused by head shaking due to an ear infection or irritation. They do occur in the Cocker Spaniel, and surgery is usually necessary.

Infection (otitis)

Due to his long, down-hanging and hairy ear flap, and consequent reduced ventilation of the ear, the Cocker Spaniel is very prone to ear infections. When otitis occurs, a smelly discharge appears, and the dog shakes his head or scratches his ear. If the inner ear is affected, the dog may also show a head tilt or a disturbance in his balance.

■ **Treatment** with antibiotic ear drops is usually successful, but sometimes syringing

STRUCTURE OF THE EAR

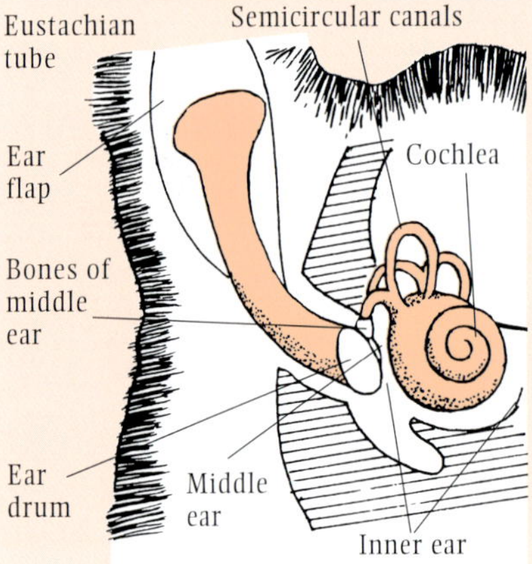

or a surgical operation is needed. The vet must be consulted as there are several possible reasons for ear disease including ear mites and grass seeds.

EYE DISEASES

Entropion

This is an inherited disease, usually of the young, growing dog, and is seen quite often in the Cocker Spaniel. The edge of an eyelid rolls inwards so that the lashes rub against the surface of the eye, causing irritation of the eyeball. The eye is sore and wet with tears, and often kept closed. Surgical treatment is necessary.

Ectropion

Also inherited, this disease is the opposite of entropion. The eyelid rolls outwards leading to a sore, very red eye. This is less common and surgery is needed to correct it.

Distichiasis

This is an inherited defect of the Cocker Spaniel in which fine extra hairs grow along the edge of the eyelid and rub against the cornea. This leads to excessive tear production and the eye looks constantly wet. These hairs are removed temporarily by plucking, or permanently by surgery.

THE EYE

Light rays pass through the cornea and pupil, and are focused by the lens on to the retina. They are then converted into nerve impulses and passed via the optic nerve to the visual cortex of the brain.

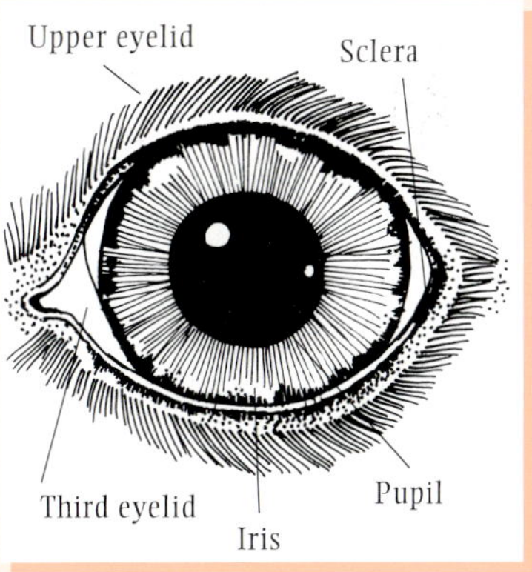

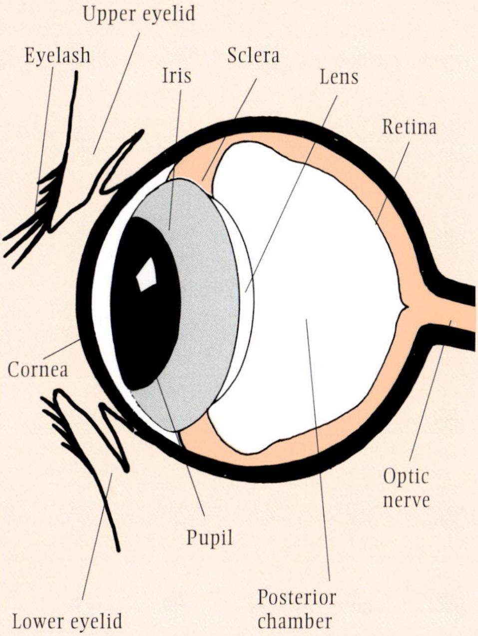

Third eyelid disease

This is usually a prolapse of the Harderian gland, a small fleshy mass of tissue behind the third eyelid. It can become displaced and protrude. Surgical removal is necessary.

Prolapse of the eye

(See first aid, page 134)

Conjunctivitis

This is common in the Cocker Spaniel. The white of the eye appears red and discharges. Possible causes include viruses, bacteria, chemicals, allergies, trauma or foreign bodies.

Keratitis

This is a very sore inflammation of the cornea which may appear blue and lose its shiny appearance.

Keratoconjunctivitis sicca (KCS)

Also known as Dry Eye, this is an autoimmune disease and is seen quite commonly in the Cocker Spaniel. It develops when the eye fails to produce tears. The cornea dries, keratitis develops, and the eye discharges a greyish sticky mucus. In time, the cornea is invaded by blood vessels which cause pigmentation and loss of sight. One or both eyes can be affected. Medical treatment can control the disease in the early stages, but KCS can cause severe loss of vision and pain.

Dermoids

A dermoid is a small surface lump on the cornea that sprouts hairs. It is a congenital defect, seen more in Cockers than in most breeds, and is present at birth. Surgical removal is necessary.

PROGRESSIVE RETINAL ATROPHY (PRA)

This is an inherited progressive degeneration of the retina of the eye which may lead to total blindness. There are two types of PRA:

- **Generalized,** which is the type usually found in the Cocker
- **Central**

Both types usually develop in the young adult. There is no treatment for PRA and the disease must be controlled by the testing of breeding dogs. Affected dogs must not be used for breeding.

Corneal ulcer

This is an erosion of part of the surface of the cornea and can follow an injury or keratitis, and is very painful. The dog will hardly be able to open his eye which will flood tears.

Pannus

This is an autoimmune inflammation of the cornea. It is known to occur in some older Cocker Spaniels.

Glaucoma

This develops when the pressure of the fluid inside the eye increases. As the pressure increases, the eye becomes painful, inflamed, and excessive tear production occurs.

- **Primary glaucoma,** an inherited defect

in some breeds.

- **Secondary glaucoma,** which follows another problem, e.g. a dislocated lens.

Persistent pupillary membrane

As the name suggests, this is a band of tissue attached to the iris which affects vision. It is inherited in the Cocker Spaniel.

Cataract

This is an opacity of the lens in one or both eyes. The pupil appears greyish instead of the normal black colour. In advanced cases, the lens looks like a pearl and the dog may be blind. Causes include infection, diabetes mellitus and trauma.

URINARY SYSTEM DISEASES

Diseases producing an increased thirst

- **Acute kidney failure**

The most common infectious agent producing acute nephritis is Leptospirosis (see infectious diseases, page 107).

- **Chronic kidney failure**

This is common in old dogs and occurs when persistent damage to the kidney results in toxic substances starting to accumulate in the bloodstream.

- **Familial nephropathy**

This is an inherited disease seen in the Cocker, whereby the kidneys fail at an early age, resulting in death. There is no treatment.

Diseases causing blood in the urine

- **Cystitis**

This is an infection of the bladder. It is more common in the bitch because the infection has easy access through the shorter urethra. The clinical signs include:

- Frequency of urination
- Straining
- Sometimes a bloody urine

In all other respects the dog remains healthy.

- **Urinary calculi or stones**

These can form in either the kidney or bladder.

- **Kidney stones** can enter the ureters, causing severe abdominal pain for the dog.
- **Bladder stones,** or calculi, are fairly common in both sexes. In the bitch, they are larger than in the dog, and straining is usually the only clinical sign. In the dog, the most common sign is unproductive straining due to urinary obstruction. This is an acute emergency.

- **Tumours of the bladder**

These occur and cause frequent straining and bloody urine, or, by occupying space within the bladder, cause incontinence.

THE MALE: URINARY SYSTEM

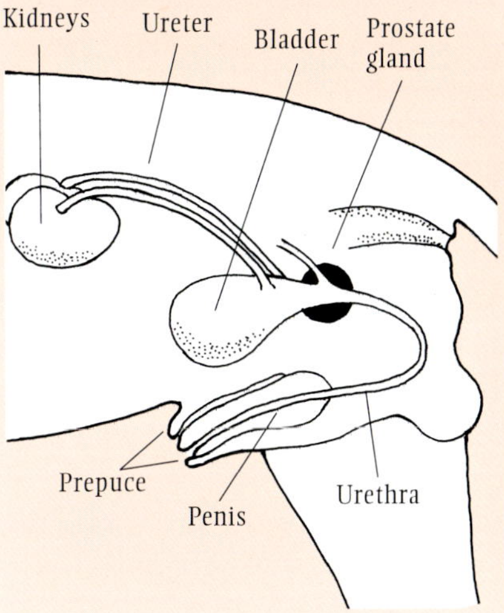

THE BITCH: URINARY SYSTEM

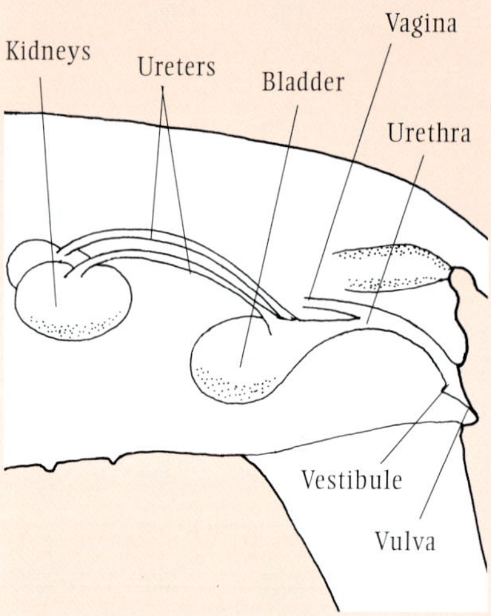

Incontinence

This occurs occasionally for no apparent reason, especially in the older bitch. Hormones or medicine to tighten the bladder sphincter can help.

Reproductive organ diseases

The male dog

■ **Retained testicle** (cryptorchidism)
Occasionally one or both testicles may fail to descend into the scrotum and remain somewhere along their developmental path in the abdomen and groin. Surgery is advisable to remove retained testicles as they are very likely to develop cancer.

■ **Tumours**
These are fairly common but, fortunately, most are benign. One type of testicular tumour, known as a Sertoli cell tumour, produces female hormones leading to the development of female characteristics.

■ **Prostate disease**
This occurs in the older Cocker Spaniel, usually a benign enlargement where the prostate slowly increases in size. Hormone treatment or castration helps.

■ **Infection of the penis and sheath** (balanitis)
An increase and discolouration occurs in the discharge from the sheath, and the dog licks his penis more frequently.

■ **Paraphimosis**
This is prolapse of the penis (see page 136).

■ **Castration**
This is of value in the treatment of behavioural problems. Excessive sexual activity, such as mounting cushions or other dogs, and territorial urination may be eliminated by castration, as may certain types of aggression and the desire to escape and wander.

The bitch

■ **Pyometra**
This uterine infection is a common and serious disease of the older bitch although bitches who have had puppies seem less likely to develop it. The treatment of choice is usually an ovariohysterectomy.

■ **Mastitis**
This is an infection of the mammary glands and occurs usually in lactating bitches. The affected glands become over-engorged, swollen, hard, and painful.

■ **Mammary tumours**
These are common in the older entire bitch. Most tumours are benign, but where malignant, they can grow rapidly and spread

THE REPRODUCTIVE SYSTEM

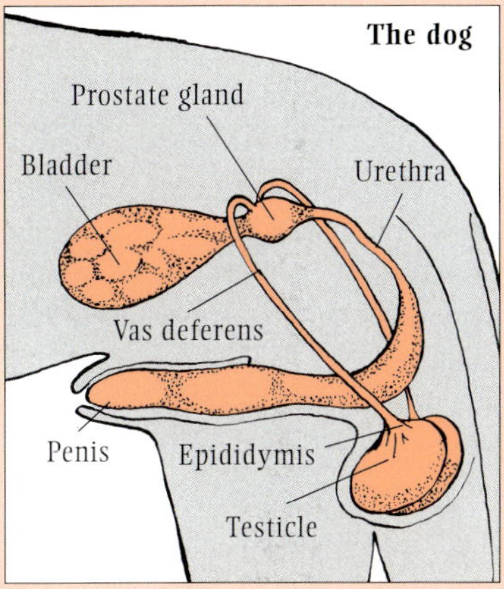

Sperm and testosterone are produced in the male dog's testicles. Sperm pass into the epididymis for storage, thence via the vas deferens during mating.

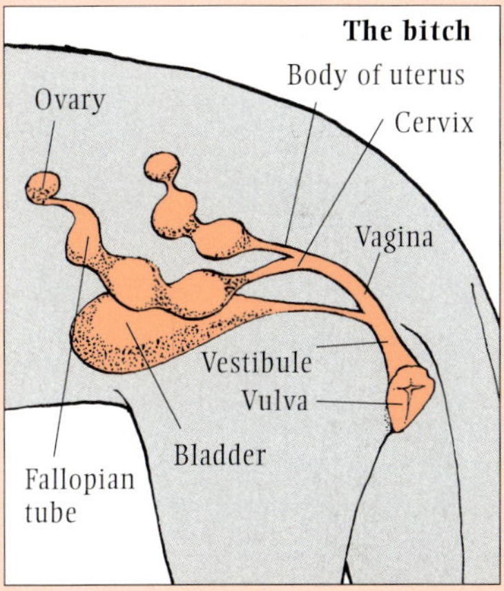

Eggs are produced in the ovaries and enter the uterus through the fallopian tubes. During the heat period, they can be fertilized by sperm.

to other organs. Early surgical removal of any lump is advisable because of the danger of malignancy.

■ **False (pseudo) pregnancy**
Once a bitch has had a false pregnancy, she is likely to have one after each heat period.

■ **Treatment,** if needed, is by hormones, and prevention is by a hormone injection, or tablets, and long term by an ovariohysterectomy.

BIRTH CONTROL

■ **Hormone therapy**
Several preparations, injections and tablets, are available to prevent or postpone the bitch's heat period.

FALSE (PSEUDO) PREGNANCY

This occurs in most bitches about eight to twelve weeks after oestrus at the stage when the bitch would be lactating had she been pregnant. The signs vary and include:

- Poor appetite
- Lethargy
- Milk production
- Nest building
- Aggressiveness
- Attachment to a substitute puppy which is often a squeaky toy

Note: Once a bitch has had a false pregnancy, she is likely to have one after each heat period.

■ **Treatment,** if needed, is by hormones, and prevention is by a hormone injection, or tablets, and long-term by an ovariohysterectomy.

■ **Spaying (ovariohysterectomy)**
This is an operation to remove the uterus and ovaries, usually performed when the bitch is not on heat. It is a good long-term solution to birth control in the bitch who will never breed.

NERVOUS SYSTEM DISEASES

The nervous system consists of two parts:

1 **The central nervous system (CNS)** The brain and the spinal cord, which runs in the vertebral column.

2 **The peripheral nervous system** All the nerves that connect the CNS to the organs of the body.

■ **Canine distemper virus**
(See page 107)

■ **Vestibular syndrome**
This is a fairly common condition of the older dog, and affects that part of the brain which controls balance. There is a sudden head tilt to the affected side, often flicking movements of the eyes called nystagmus, and the dog may fall or circle to that side. Many dogs will recover slowly but the condition may recur.

■ **Slugbait (Metaldehyde) poisoning**
The dog appears 'drunk', uncoordinated, and may have convulsions. There is no specific treatment, but sedation may lead to recovery.

■ **Epilepsy**
This is a nervous disorder causing fits. The dog has a sudden, unexpected fit or convulsion, which lasts for about two minutes. Recovery is fairly quick, although the dog may be dull and look confused for a few hours. Treatment is usually necessary and successful as far as the control of epilepsy is concerned.

BONE, MUSCLE AND JOINT DISEASES

Note: X-rays are necessary to confirm any diagnosis involving bone.

■ **Bone infection (osteomyelitis)**
This usually occurs after an injury, such as a bite, or where a broken bone protrudes through the skin. Signs are pain, heat and swelling over the site, and if a limb bone is affected, there can be severe lameness.

■ **Fractures**
Any break or crack in a bone is called a fracture. When a vet repairs a fracture, his aim is to replace the fractured ends of bone into

TYPES OF FRACTURE

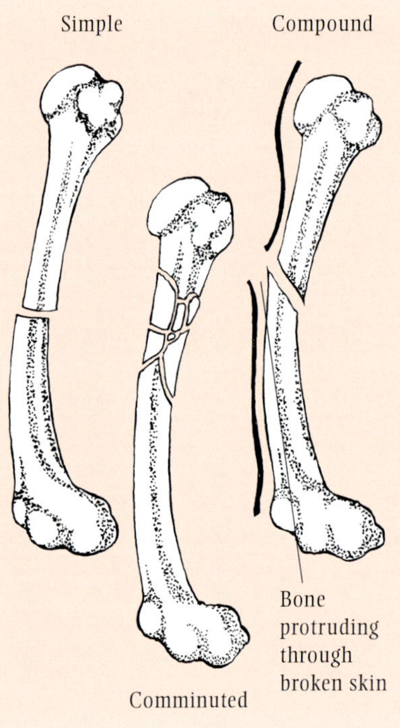

THE SKELETON

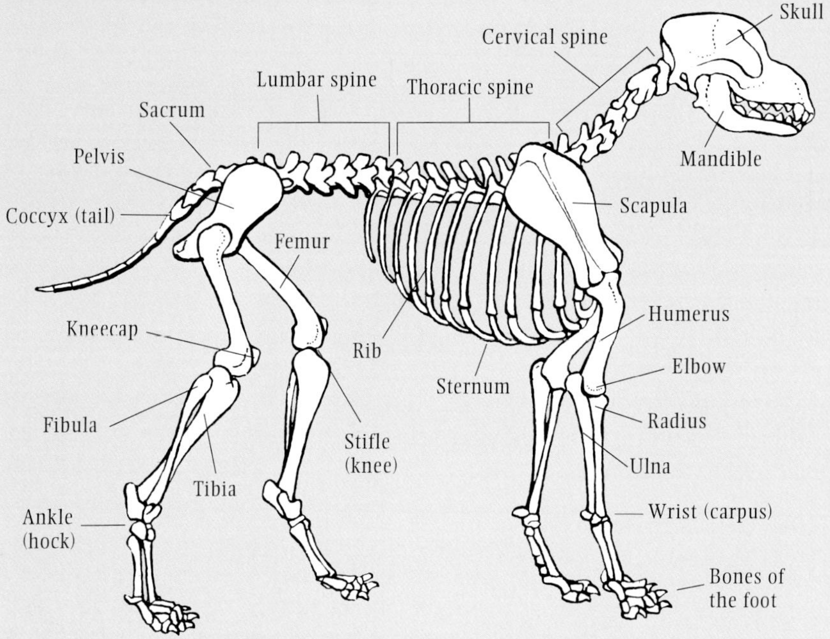

The skeleton is the framework for the body. All the dog's ligaments, muscles and tendons are attached to the bones, 319 of them in total. By a process called ossification, cartilage template is calcified to produce bone. Bones are living tissue and they respond to the stresses and strains placed upon them. To build and keep healthy bones, dogs need a nutritionally balanced diet which contains an adequate supply of calcium, vitamin D and phosphorus.

their normal position and then to immobilize the bone for four to six weeks. Depending on the bone, and type of fracture, there are several methods available.

- Cage rest
- External casts
- Surgery to perform internal fixation, e.g. by plating or pinning

■ **Bone tumours**

These are not common in the Cocker Spaniel.

■ **Sprains**

A sprain is an inflammation of an over-stretched joint. The joint is hot, swollen and painful, and the dog is lame. Allow the dog to rest and apply cold compresses to the affected area.

■ **Cruciate ligament rupture**

When the cruciate ligaments rupture, as a result of a severe sprain, the stifle or knee joint is destabilized and the dog becomes instantly and severely lame on that leg. This often occurs in middle-aged, overweight Cockers. Surgical repair is usually necessary.

■ **Hip dysplasia**

This does occasionally occur in the Cocker Spaniel and is a malformation of one or both hip joints which may not be detectable until the dog is a young adult or even older. Stiffness on rising, an odd bunny-hopping gait, or lameness are the usual signs.

■ **Arthritis or degenerative joint disease**

This occurs in the Cocker Spaniel. It results in thickening of the joint capsule, formation of abnormal new bone around the edges of the joint and, sometimes, wearing of the joint cartilage. The joint becomes enlarged and painful, and has a reduced range of movement. It tends to occur in the older dog and usually affects the hips, stifles (knees) and elbows.

■ **Spondylitis**

This is arthritis of the spine. It is not common in the Cocker Spaniel.

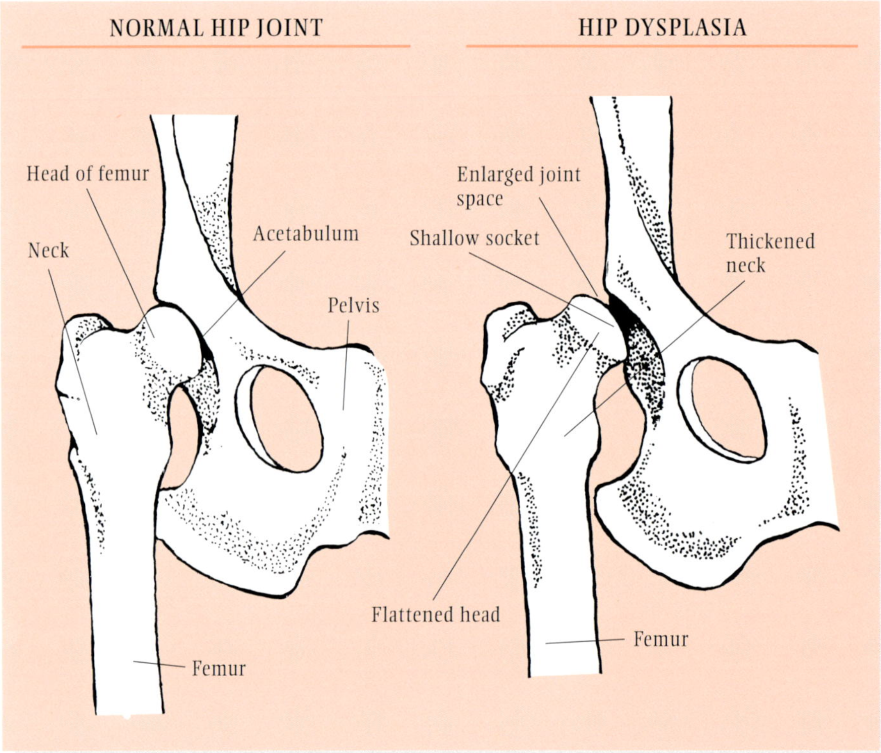

12

FIRST AID, ACCIDENTS AND EMERGENCIES

First aid is the emergency care given to a dog suffering injury or illness of sudden onset.

AIMS OF FIRST AID

1 Keep the dog alive.
2 Prevent unnecessary suffering.
3 Prevent further injury.

RULES OF FIRST AID

1

Keep calm. If you panic you will be unable to help effectively.

2

Contact a vet as soon as possible. Advice given over the telephone may be life-saving.

3

Avoid injury to yourself. A distressed or injured animal may bite so use a muzzle if necessary (see muzzling, page 136).

4

Control haemorrhage. Excessive blood loss can lead to severe shock and death (see haemorrhage, page 129),

5

Maintain an airway. Failure to breathe or obtain adequate oxygen can lead to brain damage or loss of life within five minutes (see airway obstruction and artificial respiration, page 127).

COMMON ACCIDENTS AND EMERGENCIES

The following common accidents and emergencies all require first aid action. In an emergency, your priorities are to keep the dog alive and comfortable until he can be examined by a vet. In many cases, there is effective action that you can take immediately to help preserve your dog's health and life.

Shock and road accidents

Shock

This is a serious clinical syndrome which can cause death. Shock can follow road accidents, severe burns, electrocution, extremes of heat and cold, heart failure, poisoning, severe fluid loss, reactions to drugs, insect stings or snake bite.

Signs of shock

- Weakness or collapse
- Pale gums
- Cold extremities, e.g. feet and ears
- Weak pulse and rapid heart
- Rapid, shallow breathing

Recommended action

1

Act immediately. Give cardiac massage (see page 128) and/or artificial respiration (see page 127) if necessary, after checking for a clear airway.

2

Keep the dog flat and warm. Control external haemorrhage (page 129).

3

Veterinary treatment is essential thereafter.

Road accidents

Injuries resulting from a fast-moving vehicle colliding with an animal can be very serious. Road accidents may result in:

- Death
- Head injuries
- Spinal damage
- Internal haemorrhage, bruising and rupture of major organs, e.g. liver, spleen, kidneys
- Fractured ribs and lung damage, possibly resulting in haemothorax (blood in the chest cavity) or pneumothorax (air in the chest cavity)
- Fractured limbs with or without nerve damage
- External haemorrhage, wounds, tears and bruising

Recommended action

1

Assess the situation and move the dog to a safe position. Use a blanket to transport him and keep him flat.

2

Check for signs of life: feel for a heart beat (see cardiac massage, page 128), and watch for the rise and fall of the chest wall.

3

If the dog is breathing, treat as for shock (see above). If he is not breathing but there is a heart beat, give artificial respiration, after checking for airway obstruction. Consider the use of a muzzle (see muzzling, page 136).

4

Control external haemorrhage (see haemorrhage, page 129).

5

Keep the dog warm and flat at all times, and seek veterinary help.

AIRWAY OBSTRUCTION

■ **FOREIGN BODY IN THE THROAT,** e.g. a ball.

RECOMMENDED ACTION

1

This is an acute emergency. Do not try to pull out the object. Push it upwards and forwards from behind the throat so that it moves from its position, where it is obstructing the larynx, into the mouth.

2

The dog should now be able to breathe. Remove the object from his mouth.

■ **FOLLOWING A ROAD ACCIDENT,** or convulsion, blood, saliva or vomit in the throat may obstruct breathing.

RECOMMENDED ACTION

1

Pull the tongue forwards and clear any obstruction with your fingers.

2

Then, with the dog on his side, extend the head and neck forwards to maintain a clear airway.

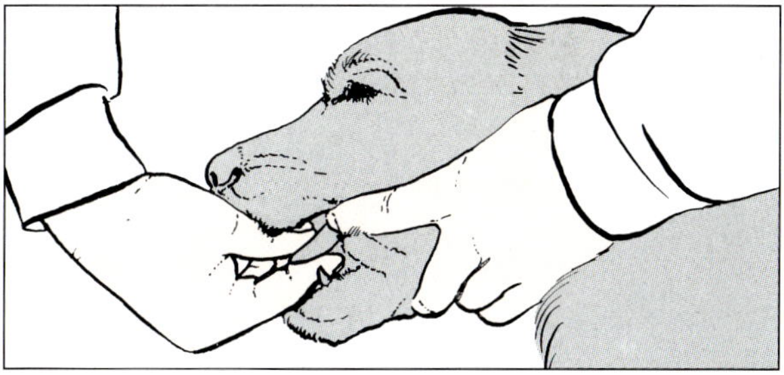

DROWNING

RECOMMENDED ACTION

1

Out of water, remove the collar and place the dog on his side with his head lower than his body.

2

With hands, apply firm downward pressure on chest at five-second intervals.

ARTIFICIAL RESPIRATION

This is the method for helping a dog which has a clear airway but cannot breathe.

RECOMMENDED ACTION

Use mouth-to-mouth resuscitation by cupping your hands over his nose and mouth and blowing into his nostrils every five seconds.

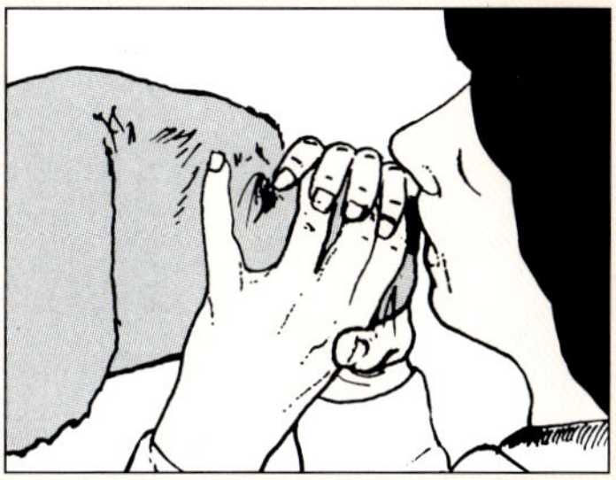

CARDIAC MASSAGE

This is required if your dog's heart fails.

RECOMMENDED ACTION

1

With the dog lying on his right side, feel for a heart beat with your fingers on the chest wall behind the dog's elbows on his left side.

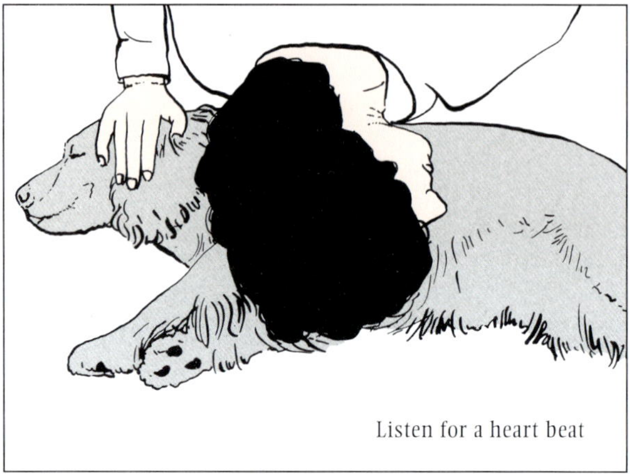

Listen for a heart beat

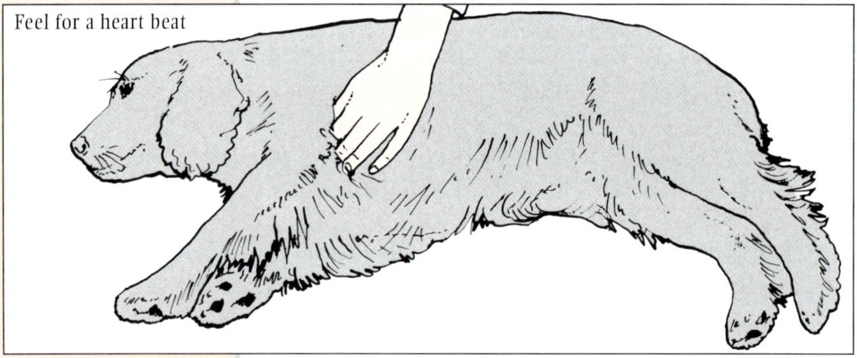

Feel for a heart beat

2

If you feel nothing, squeeze rhythmically with your palms, placing one hand on top of the other, as shown, at two-second intervals, pressing down hard.

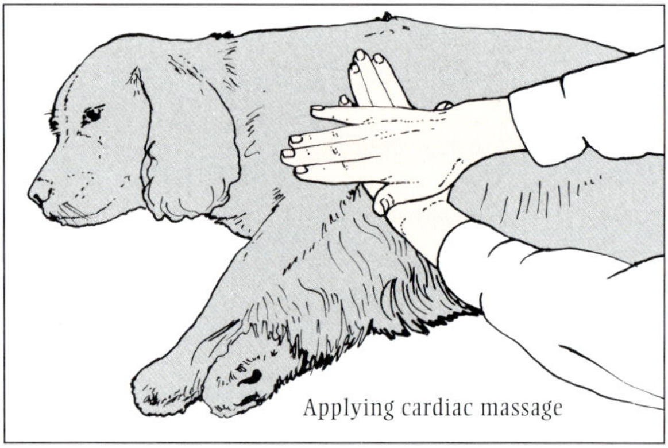

Applying cardiac massage

Haemorrhage

Severe haemorrhage must be controlled, as it leads to a precipitous fall in blood pressure and the onset of shock. Haemorrhage is likely to result from deep surface wounds, or internal injuries, e.g. following a road accident.

■ **For surface wounds**

Recommended action

Locate the bleeding point and apply pressure either with:

■ **Your thumb** or

■ **A pressure bandage** (preferred method) or

■ **A tourniquet**

1 **Pressure bandage**
Use a pad of gauze, cotton wool or cloth against the wound and tightly bandage around it. In the absence of a proper dressing, use a clean handkerchief or scarf.

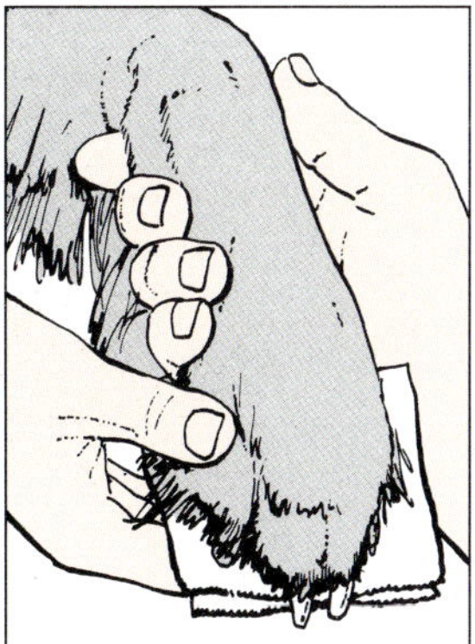

1 Pressure bandage

2 If the bleeding continues, apply another dressing on top of the first.

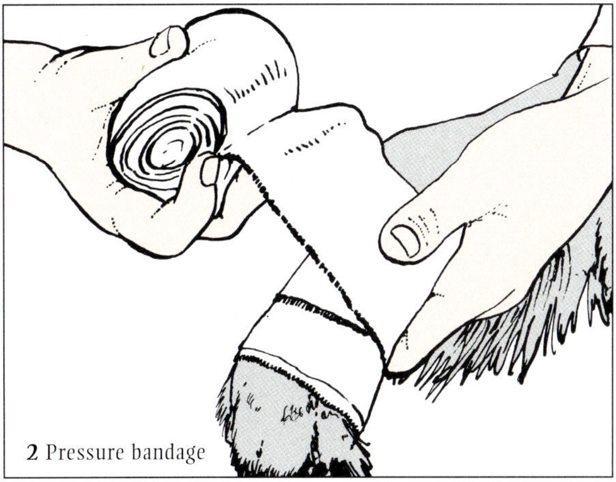

2 Pressure bandage

1 **Tourniquet**
(on limbs and tail)
Tie a narrow piece of cloth, a neck tie or dog lead tightly around the limb, nearer to the body than the wound itself.

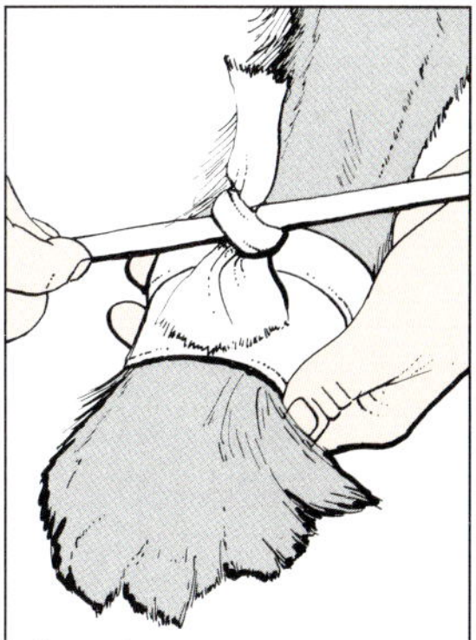

Tourniquet

2 Using a pencil or stick within the knot, twist until it becomes tight enough to stop the blood flow.

3 **Important**: you must seek veterinary assistance as soon as possible.

Note: Tourniquets should be applied for no longer than fifteen minutes at a time, or tissue death may result.

■ **For internal bleeding**

Recommended action

1 You should keep the animal quiet and warm, and minimize any movement.

2 **Important**: you must seek veterinary assistance as soon as possible.

WOUNDS

These may result from road accidents, dog fights, sharp stones or glass, etc. Deep wounds may cause serious bleeding, bone or nerve damage.

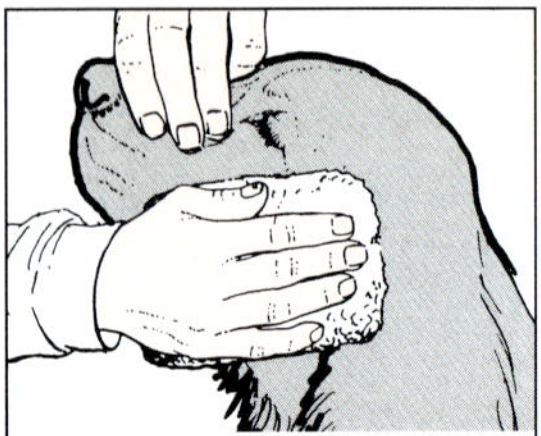

1 Bathe the wound

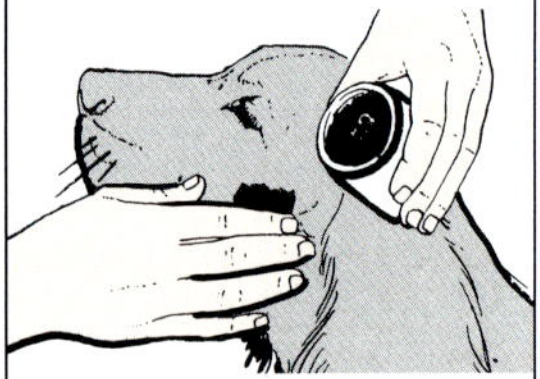

2 Apply antiseptic cream

RECOMMENDED ACTION

1

Deal with external bleeding (see haemorrhage, page 129) and keep the dog quiet before seeking veterinary attention.

2

Cut feet or pads should be bandaged to prevent further blood loss.

3

Minor cuts, abrasions and bruising should be bathed with warm salt solution (one 5ml teaspoonful per 550ml (1 pint) of water). They should be protected from further injury or contamination. Apply some antiseptic cream, if necessary.

4

If in doubt, ask your vet to check in case the wound needs suturing or antibiotic therapy, particularly if caused by fighting. Even minor cuts and punctures can be complicated by the presence of a foreign body.

FRACTURES

Broken bones, especially in the legs, often result from road accidents. Be careful when lifting and transporting the affected dog.

■ **LEG FRACTURES**

RECOMMENDED ACTION

1 Broken lower leg bones can sometimes be straightened gently, bandaged and then taped or tied with string to a makeshift splint, e.g. a piece of wood or rolled-up newspaper or cardboard.

2 Otherwise, support the leg to prevent any movement. Take the dog to the vet immediately.

■ **OTHER FRACTURES**

These may be more difficult to diagnose. If you suspect a fracture, transport your dog very gently with great care, and get him to the vet.

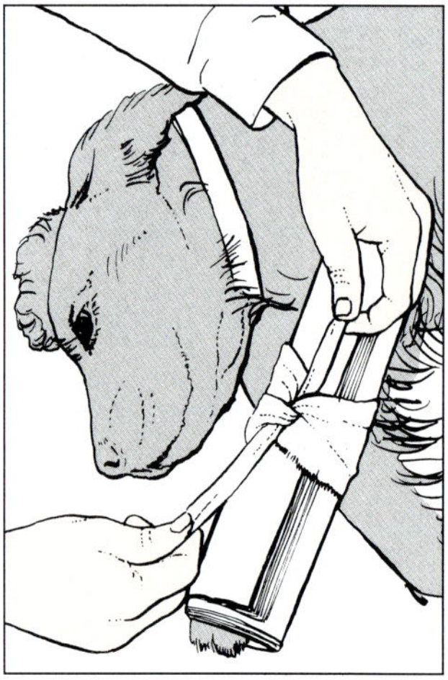

OTHER ACCIDENTS AND EMERGENCIES

COLLAPSE

This may be accompanied by loss of consciousness, but not in every case.

POSSIBLE CAUSES

- Head trauma, e.g. following a road accident
- Heart failure
- Stroke
- Hyperthermia (heat stroke)
- Hypothermia (cold)
- Hypocalcaemia (low calcium)
- Shock
- Spinal fractures
- Asphyxia (interference with breathing)
- Electrocution
- Poisoning

Note: you should refer to the relevant section for further details of these problems.

RECOMMENDED ACTION

1 The collapsed animal must be moved with care to avoid further damage.

2 Gently slide him on his side onto a blanket or coat.

3 Check he is breathing, and then keep him quiet and warm until you obtain professional help.

4 If he is not breathing, administer artificial respiration immediately, after checking for a clear airway (see page 127).

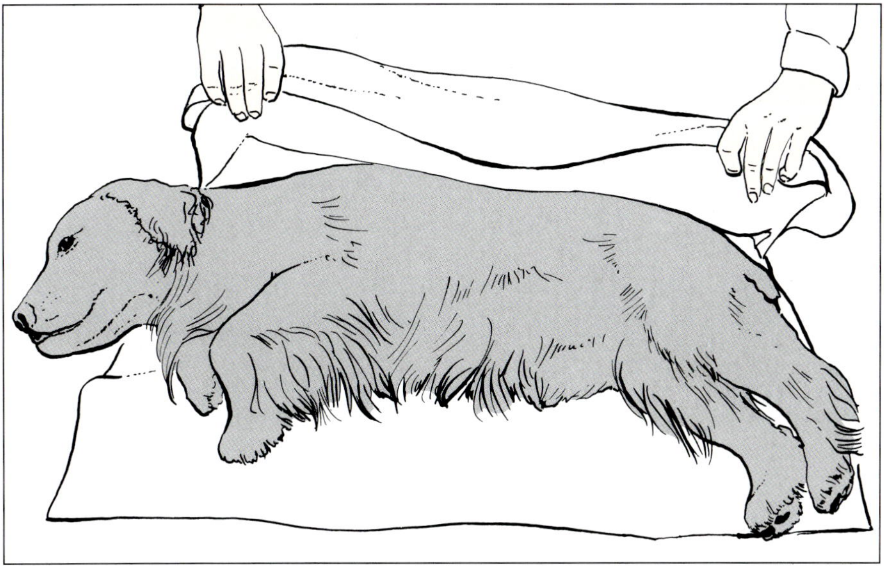

CONVULSIONS (FITS OR SEIZURES)

These are very alarming to dog owners. Uncontrolled spasms, 'paddling' of legs, loss of consciousness, sometimes salivation and involuntary urination or defecation occur. Most convulsions only last a few minutes, but the dog is often confused and dazed afterwards.

POSSIBLE CAUSES

- Poisoning
- Head injuries
- Brain tumours
- Liver and kidney disease
- Meningitis
- Epilepsy
- Low blood glucose, e.g. in diabetes, or low blood calcium, e.g. in eclampsia

RECOMMENDED ACTION

1 Unless he is in a dangerous situation, do not attempt to hold the dog, but protect him from damaging himself.

2 Do not give him anything by mouth.

3 Try to keep him quiet, cool and in a darkened room until he sees the vet.

4 If you have to move him, cover him with a blanket first.

HEART FAILURE

This is not as common in dogs as in humans. Affected dogs faint, usually during exercise, and lose consciousness. The mucous membranes appear pale or slightly blue.

RECOMMENDED ACTION

1 Cover the dog in a blanket, and lie him on his side.

2 Massage his chest behind the elbows (see cardiac massage, page 128).

3 When he recovers, take him straight to the vet.

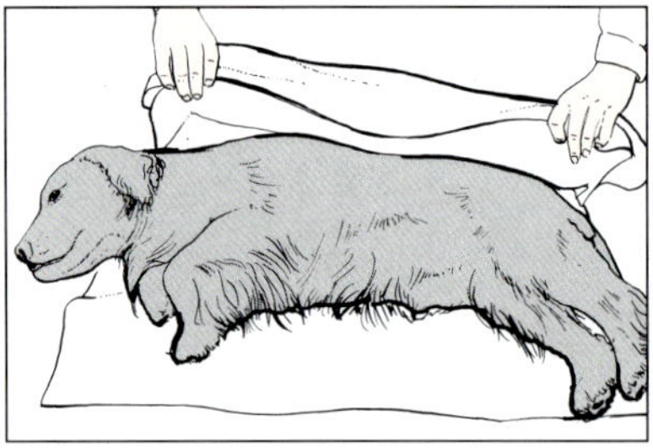

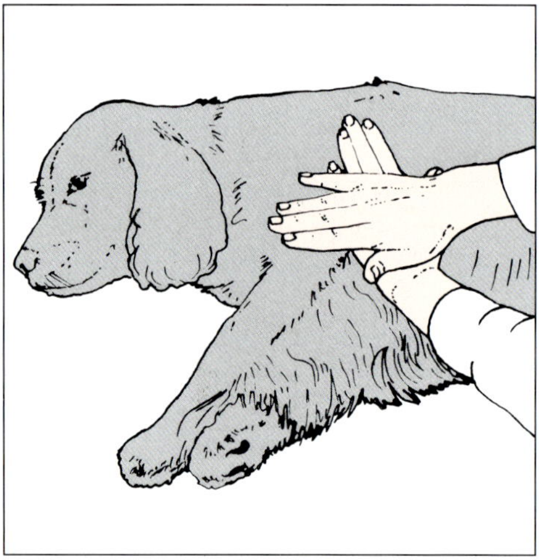

1 An affected dog should be covered with a blanket and laid on his side.

2 Apply cardiac massage, pressing down firmly at two-second intervals.

HEAT-STROKE

This occurs in hot weather, especially when dogs have been left in cars with insufficient ventilation. Affected animals are extremely distressed, panting and possibly collapsed. They can die rapidly. A heat-stroke case should be treated as an acute emergency.

RECOMMENDED ACTION

1 Place the dog in a cold bath or run cold water over his body until his temperature is in the normal range.

2 Offer water with added salt (one 5ml teaspoonful per half litre/18 fl oz water).

3 Treatment for shock may be necessary (see page 126).

ELECTROCUTION

This is most likely to occur in a bored puppy who chews through a cable. Electrocution may kill him outright or lead to delayed shock.

- **DO NOT TOUCH HIM BEFORE YOU SWITCH OFF THE ELECTRICITY SOURCE.**

RECOMMENDED ACTION

1 If he is not breathing, begin artificial respiration immediately (see page 127) and keep him warm.

2 Contact your vet; if he survives he will need treatment for shock (see page 126).

BURNS AND SCALDS

POSSIBLE CAUSES

- Spilled hot drinks, boiling water or fat.
- Friction, chemical and electrical burns.

RECOMMENDED ACTION

1 Immediately apply running cold water and, thereafter, cold compresses, ice packs or packets of frozen peas to the affected area.

2 Veterinary attention is essential in most cases.

SNAKE BITE

This is due to the adder in Great Britain. Signs are pain accompanied by a soft swelling around two puncture wounds, usually on either the head, neck or limbs. Trembling, collapse, shock and even death can ensue.

RECOMMENDED ACTION

1 Do not let the dog walk; carry him to the car.

2 Keep him warm, and take him immediately to the vet.

FOREIGN BODIES

■ **IN THE MOUTH**
Sticks or bones wedged between the teeth cause frantic pawing at the mouth and salivation.

RECOMMENDED ACTION

Remove the foreign body with your fingers or pliers, using a wooden block placed between the dog's canine teeth if possible to aid the safety of this procedure. Some objects have to be removed under general anaesthesia.
Note: a ball in the throat is dealt with in airway obstruction (see page 127), and is a critical emergency.

■ **FISH HOOKS**
Never try to pull these out, wherever they are.

RECOMMENDED ACTION

Cut the end with pliers and then push the barbed end through the skin and out.

■ **IN THE EAR – GRASS SEEDS**
These are the little spiky seeds of the wild barley, and are a real nuisance to Cocker Spaniels with their long, floppy ears, and long coat. If one finds its way into an ear, it can produce sudden severe distress and violent head shaking.

RECOMMENDED ACTION

If you can see the seed, gently but firmly pull it out with tweezers, and check it is intact. If you cannot see it, or feel you may have left some in, call the vet immediately.

■ **IN THE FOOT**
Glass, thorns or splinters can penetrate the pads or soft skin, causing pain, and infection if neglected.

RECOMMENDED ACTION

Soak the foot in warm salt water and then use a sharp sterilized needle or pair of tweezers to extract the foreign body. If this is not possible, take your dog to the vet who will remove it under local or general anaesthetic if necessary.

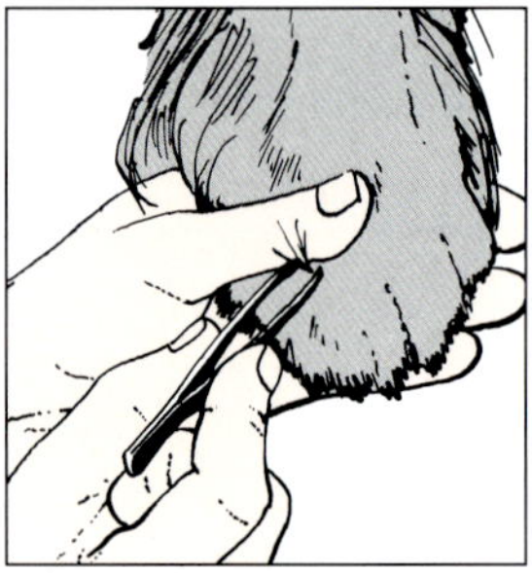

NOSE BLEEDS

These may be caused by trauma or violent sneezing, but are also related in some cases to ulceration of the lining of the nasal cavity.

RECOMMENDED ACTION

1 Keep the dog quiet and use ice packs on the nose.

2 Contact your vet if the bleeding persists.

EYEBALL PROLAPSE

Not a common problem in Cocker Spaniels, but may arise from head trauma, e.g. following a dog fight. The eye is forced out of its socket and sight is lost unless it is replaced within fifteen minutes.

RECOMMENDED ACTION

1 Speed is essential. One person should pull the eyelids apart while the other gently presses the eyeball back into its socket, using moist sterile gauze or cloth.

2 If this is impossible, cover the eye with moist sterile gauze and take him to your vet immediately.

Gastric dilation

This is an emergency and cannot be treated at home. The stomach distends with gas and froth which the dog cannot easily eliminate. In some cases, the stomach then rotates and a torsion occurs, so the gases cannot escape at all and the stomach rapidly fills the abdomen. This causes pain, respiratory distress and circulatory failure. Life-threatening shock follows. It is a very rare condition in the Cocker Spaniel.

Preventive action

1 Avoid the problem by not exercising your dog vigorously for two hours after a full meal.

2 If your dog is becoming bloated and has difficulty breathing, he is unlikely to survive unless he has veterinary attention within half an hour of the onset of symptoms, so get him to the vet immediately.

Poisoning

Dogs can be poisoned by pesticides, herbicides, poisonous plants, paints, antifreeze or an overdose of drugs (animal or human).

- If poisoning is suspected, first try to determine the agent involved, and find out if it is corrosive or not. This may be indicated on the container, but may also be evident from the blistering of the lips, gums and tongue, and increased salivation.

Recommended action

- **Corrosive poisons**

1 Wash the inside of the dog's mouth.

2 Give him milk and bread to protect the gut against the effects of the corrosive.

3 Seek veterinary help.

- **Other poisons**

1 If the dog is conscious, make him vomit within half an hour of taking the poison.

2 A crystal of washing soda or a few 15ml tablespoonfuls of strong salt solution can be given carefully by mouth.

3 Retain a sample of vomit to aid identification of the poison, or take the poison container with you to show the vet. There may be a specific antidote, and any information can help in treatment.

Stings

Bee and wasp stings often occur around the head, front limbs or mouth. The dog usually shows sudden pain and paws at, or licks, the stung area. A soft, painful swelling appears; sometimes the dog seems unwell or lethargic. Stings in the mouth and throat can be distressing and dangerous.

Recommended action

1 Withdraw the sting (bees).

2 Then you can bathe the area in:

- Vinegar for wasps
- Bicarbonate for bees

3 An antihistamine injection may be needed.

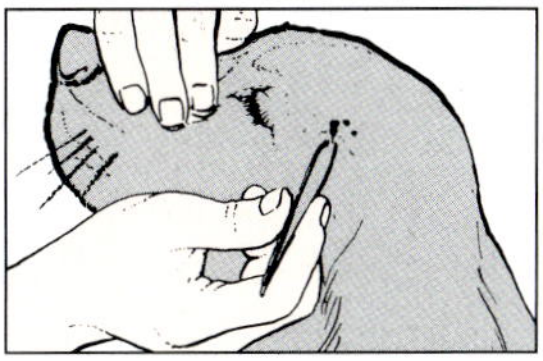

BREEDING

ECLAMPSIA

This is an emergency which may occur when your Cocker Spaniel bitch is suckling puppies, usually when the pups are about three weeks old.

PARAPHIMOSIS

(See page 120)

This problem may occur after mating, in the male Cocker Spaniel. His engorged penis is unable to retract into the sheath.

MUZZLING

This will allow a nervous, distressed or injured dog to be examined safely, without the risk of being bitten. A tape or bandage is secured around the muzzle as illustrated. However, a muzzle should not be applied in the following circumstances:

- Airway obstruction
- Loss of consciousness
- Compromised breathing or severe chest injury

1 Tie a knot in the bandage.

2 Wrap around the dog's muzzle with the knot under the lower jaw.

3 Tie firmly behind the dog's head.

1

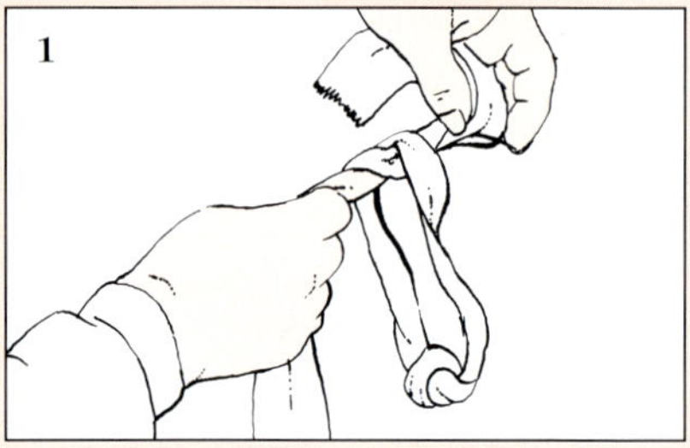

2

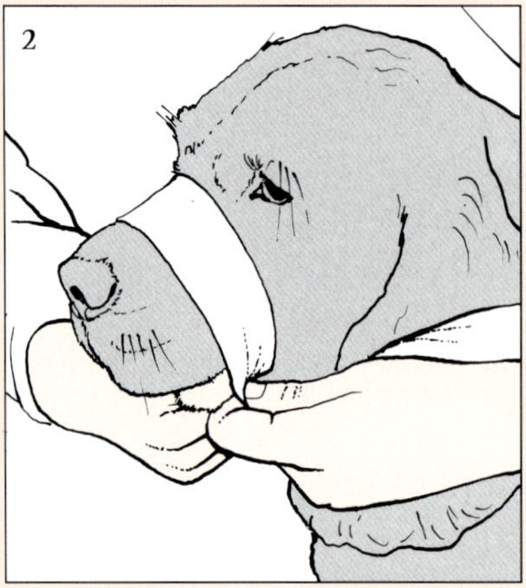

3

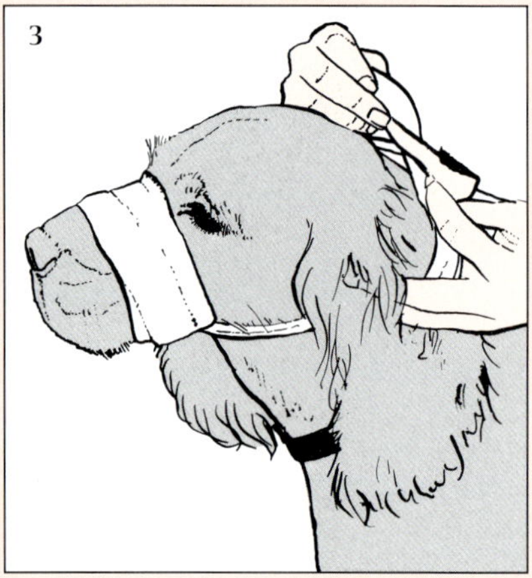

GLOSSARY

Angulation
The angles created by bones meeting at a joint.

Breed standard
The description laid down by the Kennel Club of the perfect breed specimen.

Brood bitch
A female dog which is used for breeding.

Carpals
These are the wrist bones.

Croup
This is the dog's rump: the front of the pelvis to the start of the tail.

Dam
The mother of puppies.

Dew claw
A fifth toe above the ground on the inside of the legs.

Elbow
The joint at the top of the forearm below the upper arm.

Flank
The area between the last rib and hip on the side of the body.

Furnishings
The long hair on the head, legs, thighs, back of buttocks or tail.

Gait
How a dog moves at different speeds.

Guard hairs
Long hairs that grow through the undercoat.

Muzzle
The foreface, or front of the head.

Occiput
The back upper part of the skull.

Oestrus
The periods when a bitch is 'on heat' or 'in season' and responsive to mating.

Pastern
Between the wrist (carpus) and the digits of the forelegs.

Scissor bite
Strong jaws with upper teeth overlapping lower ones.

Stifle
The hind leg joint, or 'knee'.

Undercoat
A dense, short coat hidden below the top-coat.

Whelping
The act of giving birth.

Whelps
Puppies that have not been weaned.

Whiskers
Long hairs on the jaw and muzzle.

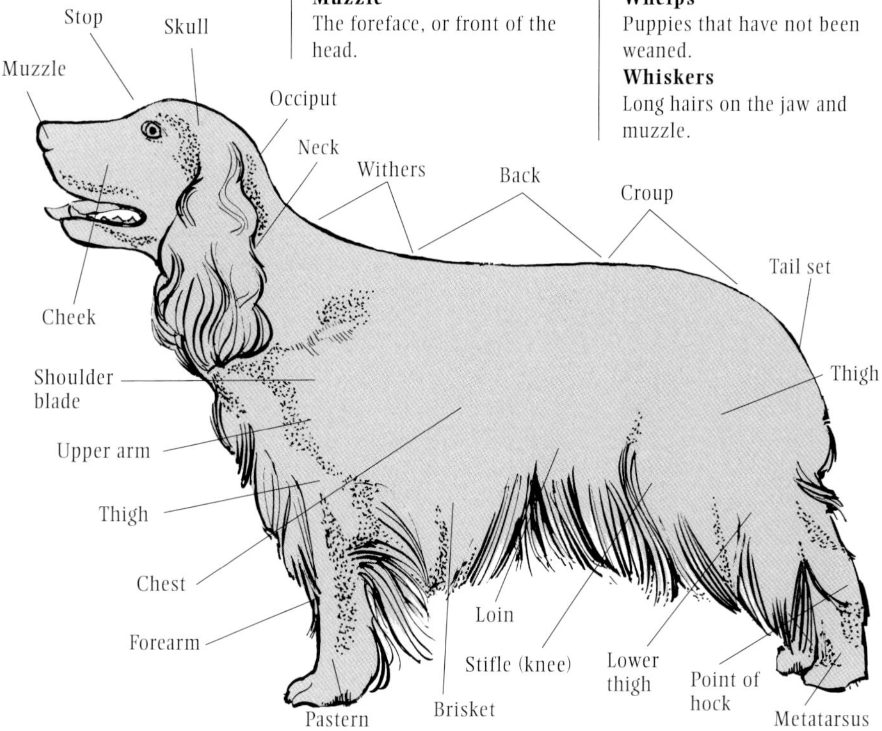

INDEX

E

F

U

V

W

Z

FURTHER READING (PERIODICALS)

Dogs Monthly
R T C Associates, Ascot House
High Street, Ascot
Berks SL5 7JG

Dogs Today
Pet Subjects Ltd
Pankhurst Farm, Bagshot Road
West End, Nr Woking
Surrey GU24 9QR

Dog Training Weekly
4/5 Feidr Castell Business
Park,
Fishguard
Dyfed SA65 9BB

Dog World
9 Tufton Street
Ashford, Kent TN23 IQN

Our Dogs
5 Oxford Road,
Station Approach
Manchester M60 ISX

Useful Addresses

Animal Aunts
Wydnooch,
45 Fairview Rd
Headley Down
Hampshire
GU38 8HQ
(Home sitters, holidays)

Animal Studies Centre,
Waltham-on-the-Wolds
Melton Mowbray
Leics LE14 4RS
(Animal nutrition)

Association of Pet Behaviour Counsellors
257 Royal College Street
London
NW1 9LU

British Veterinary Association
7 Mansfield Street
London W1M 0AT

Dog Breeders Insurance Co Ltd
9 St Stephens Court
St Stephens Road
Bournemouth
BH2 6LG
(Books of cover notes for dog breeders)

Featherbed Country Club,
High Wycombe,
Bucks.
(Luxury dog accommodation)

Guide Dogs for the Blind Association
Hillfield
Burghfield
Reading
RG7 3YG

Hearing Dogs for the Deaf
The Training Centre
London Road
Lewknor
Oxon OX9 5RY

Home Sitters
Buckland Wharf
Buckland
Aylesbury
Bucks HP22 5LO

The Kennel Club
1-5 Clarges Street,
Piccadilly
London
W1Y 8AB
(Breed Standards, Breed Club and Field Trial contact addresses, registration forms, Good Citizen training scheme)

The London Cocker
Spaniel Society
Mr R W Crisp
192 Westmorland Ave
Limbury, Luton
Beds LU3 2PU

National Canine Defence League
1 & 2 Pratt Mews
London
NW1 0AD

Pets As Therapy (PAT Dogs)
6 New Road,
Ditton
Kent ME20 6AD
(Information: how friendly dogs can join the hospital visiting scheme)

PRO Dogs National Charity
4 New Road, Ditton
Kent
ME20 6AD
(Information: Better British Breeders, worming certificates to provide with puppies, how to cope with grief on the loss of a loved dog etc.)

Royal Society for the Prevention of Cruelty to Animals
RSPCA Headquarters
Causeway
Horsham
West Sussex
RH12 1HG

SCAMPERS SCHOOL FOR DOGS

Scampers helps to train over 200 dogs and puppies every week, using kind, reward-based methods and behaviour therapy, in its unique indoor training facilities. Expert advice is given on all aspects of dog care, and there are puppy, beginners, intermediate and advanced classes. Scampers also run courses for other dog trainers and people interested in a career in dog training.

Scampers Pet Products
This specialist mail order service provides special products, including books, videos, toys, accessories and training equipment, for dog owners. It is based at Scampers Petcare Superstore, which offers one of the largest ranges of dog accessories in the UK. For more information on Scampers School for Dogs, Scampers Petcare Superstore or Scampers Pet Products contact:

Scampers Petcare Superstore
Northfield Road
Soham
Nr. Ely
Cambs CB7 5UF
Tel: 01353 720431
Fax: 01353 624202